UNS*UCK YOURSELF!

The Guide to Designing a Life You Love

SAMANTHA BUCKLEY-HUGESSEN

©2019

Copyright © 2019 Samantha Buckley-Hugessen

UNS*UCK YOURSELF!

All rights reserved. No part of this publication may be reproduced, distributed, or transmitted in any form or by any means, including photocopying, recording, or other electronic or mechanical methods, without the prior written permission of the publisher, except in the case of brief quotations embodied in critical reviews and certain other noncommercial uses permitted by copyright law. For permission requests, write to the publisher, addressed "Attention: Permissions Coordinator," at info@beyondpublishing.net

Quantity sales special discounts are available on quantity purchases by corporations, associations, and others. For details, contact the publisher at the address above.

Orders by U.S. trade bookstores and wholesalers. Email info@BeyondPublishing.net

The Beyond Publishing Speakers Bureau can bring authors to your live event. For more information or to book an event contact the Beyond Publishing Speakers Bureau speak@BeyondPublishing.net

The Author can be reached directly BeyondPublishing.net/AuthorSamanthaBuckley-Hugessen

Samantha Buckley Hugessen
Master Certified Professional Coach, Mentor and Trainer
Cabo Cell (624) 191-2090; Cabo office (624)131-5780
Facebook: Samantha Buckley Hugessen A Designed Life, LLC
Twitter: A Designed Life
Skype: adesignedlife
www.linkedin.com
Web: http://adesignedlifellc.com

Manufactured and printed in the United States of America distributed globally by BeyondPublishing.net

New York | Los Angeles | London | Sydney

ISBN Hardcover: 978-1-949873-08-5

ISBN Softcover: 978-1-947256-35-4

Dedication

To my clients that helped me learn how to best help the world get unstuck.

ACKNOWLEDGMENTS

Thank you, Kim and Juanita from RTI publishing for putting up with me while I tried to get my voice into these pages.

Mary Morrisey, you taught me the universal laws in a way that I could really hear and understand.

I even will say thank you to my husband Alex, even though he thinks it's all Woo-Woo stuff, he totally supports me anyway.

Michael at Beyond Publishing for being so enthusiastic about this book.

Finally, my kids Kai and Jack for thinking I am the best mom and the coolest ever for writing a book.

FOREWORD

On December 3, 2012, I somewhat reluctantly prepped my then-baby for bed and shuffled out the door to attend a business workshop. I had read a Facebook ad that was promoting a 'town center' style get-together for entrepreneurs and I had confirmed my attendance. At that time, I had a relatively new business and was two years into my first foray at motherhood. I was aware that I had no clue what I was doing in either field of life and felt drawn to being a part of this meeting.

Back then, I had no life strategies in place - all I knew was that I had to keep myself together for my baby and come up with enough money to pay my half of our household bills. I didn't know how to grow a business other than working myself to the bone.

I thought that life was supposed to be hard. I thought that earning money was never meant to be easy. I thought that in order to be successful, I had to dedicate most of my days to blood, sweat and tears.

Ultimately, I was curious to attend a public event that could shed some light on what kind of life I was supposed to be living. That workshop was held by Samantha Buckley-Hugessen. I had never heard of Samantha before, but within an hour of that meeting beginning, I was mesmerized.

I nervously entered the workshop and was quickly seated amongst other locals who all came to listen and learn. I had expectations of being talked at for an hour; little did I know I was actually going to have to do some work of my own. Samantha was sharing a concept I had never heard of before: that I could design my own life around my passions and desires.

Nobody had ever given me permission to design my days around personal fulfillment, family time and doing work that I loved. The concept of easily earning an income without having to bust a gut in the process seemed like a complete fallacy.

That is until I heard what Samantha had to say that fateful evening.

By 8 pm, I left the workshop armed with my first ever life plan and a feeling of reassurance that I could not just handle everything that was happening in my life but thrive at the same time.

That meeting was to be the start of many years of personal and professional mentorship between Samantha and me.

Samantha is a force to be reckoned with.

It's rare to meet someone who is as excited about getting you on your best track as you might be for yourself.

I've been lucky to attend numerous workshops, coaching sessions and small-group masterminds with Samantha since then. The beauty of her work is that rarely does she preach. Instead, she questions, gently probes and encourages you to reposition your own life. Perhaps most importantly, Samantha impresses upon you that your life is a blank canvas that YOU alone create.

Ultimately, Samantha not only gives you permission to dream, she teaches you how to do it again.

Full disclosure - Samantha's systemized coaching doesn't allow for excuses. There's no room for the blame game or festering in your own woes. Sure, there's an acknowledgment of life events, but at the core of it all - Samantha is a truth-seeker.

She's looking for you to find YOUR truth.

No stone goes unturned as she supports you in your journey of self-inquiry.

Rarely do we allow ourselves to dream and even rarer still do we take note of those dreams. Isn't it true that from an early age, we are told to STOP day-dreaming? In school we're told to accept our circumstances as fact and get on with life as best we can. Samantha's work gave me a chance to evaluate my life and create an internal vision board of sorts that I can refer back to and stay the course.

Fast-forward to 2019, where I now live that life that I dreamed of so many years ago. Of course, the way that I have designed my life probably looks completely different to what your dream life might look like, but I'm forever in debt to the woman who told me I had a big fat green light to do whatever I wanted in my professional life.

Along the way, there have been extreme highs and lows, as one might expect in the world of business, but the biggest reward of it all is that I'm living an authentic version of life on my own terms.

As a serial female entrepreneur, it can be challenging to find a personal and professional compass. As a mother of small children, trying her best to navigate both personal and professional successes and failures, it becomes imperative to seek direction and support from an individual who can see through the paradigms that you aren't aware that you even have. Samantha came into my life when I couldn't put my finger on what I needed, yet brought me such an invaluable gift.

I'm proud to have her as my life coach and even more proud to call her a dear friend.

If you're seeking clarity, then do the work within the pages of this book.

Invest some time into the divine planning of your life, for there's no time to lose and no better place to start.

We all deserve to live a life that we love.

Jenni Reichert

TABLE OF CONTENTS

Dedication 3
Acknowledgments 4
Foreword 7
Table of Contents 11
Chapter 1: Being Stuck Sucks 15
    One Decision Can Make All the Difference 20
    Are You Stuck? 21
    Signs That You Are Stuck 21
    Okay, You Got Me, I'm Stuck. Now What? 28

Chapter 2: Grand Overall Designer 31
    Faith 37

Chapter 3: Fluid Thinking 43
    Conditions and Circumstances 43
    Let's Get Started 44
    Dream It Up 44
    Exercise #1 45
    Sandra's Story 49
    Exercise: Write Out Your Future 50
    Vision Exercise: Crafting the Life You LOVE 51

Chapter 4: Come Back From the Future 61
    What If? 61
    Symptoms You're Living in the Future 67
    Changing "How" to "What's next?" 69
    Lisa and Her Dream 70
    The Only Time is Now 71
    Stop Waiting for Five Million-Dollar Ideas 73
    Ask the Question, Take the Action 73

Chapter 5: The Past is the Past, Let's Leave it There — 75

    The Value of the Past: Reflection — 76
    The Problems with Living in the Past — 77
    Look for the Lesson — 78
    Past Memories Hurt Present Relationships — 81
    Larry's Story — 81
    Suffering is (kinda) Selfish — 83
    Exercise: Step into the Present — 84
    Start Where You Are — 85

Chapter 6: The Only Time is Now — 87

    The Lean-In Approach — 89
    Lean In: Crisis Time — 92
    Take the Charge Out of the Situation — 93
    Lean into the Fear — 94
    The Man Who Sold Very Good Hot Dogs — 97
    J.K. Rowling — 98
    Procrastination Paralyzes — 99

Chapter 7: Do You Really Know? — 103

    Watch Out for the Know-It-All — 105
    Faith in Action — 107
    Practice True Knowing Today — 108

Chapter 8: The Power of Belief — 111

Chapter 9: You Can Start Right Now — 121

    Get a PIMP — 123
    Gratitude — 125
    Meditation — 126
    Breathing Exercises — 126
    Intention and Affirmation — 127
    Visualization — 130
    Journaling — 132
    Consistency — 134

Chapter 10: The Key to Life: Gratitude — 137

    Research on Gratitude — 138
    Two Types of Gratitude — 139
    The Science of Happiness — 144
    Think It and Ink it — 147

    Gratitude Exercise Review … 147
Chapter 11: The Road Ahead … **149**
    A Bump in the Road … 149
    Defuse the Disconnect … 154
    The Accountability Advantage … 155
Chapter 12: So, What Do You Know? … **159**
    LOVE/NOT IT … 161
Your Vision Story … **161**

CHAPTER 1
BEING STUCK SUCKS

> *If you want small changes in your life, work on your attitude. But if you want big and primary changes, work on your paradigm.*
> **Stephen Covey**

"This sucks," I thought to myself; and it wasn't for the first time, either. For months now, I could feel it growing stronger and stronger inside of me, and I wasn't sure how much more I could take. Here I was, in my early 20s, and instead of living life to the fullest, I was stressed, depressed, and beginning to feel hopeless. Life was hard and wasn't getting any easier, it seemed.

Here's the deal: I hid it from everybody. It all looked good on the outside. A 6'2" blonde in a high-powered job, rocking the career goals, and making good money—I was a powerhouse. From the outside, my life looked pretty sweet, but on the inside, I was struggling. I wasn't living. I was *surviving*, doing my damnedest to get out from under, fighting from the inside out. I knew that life could and should be better. Life was hard, but I was tired of surviving. There's no joy in that, no life in that. I wanted to *thrive*.

I was raised (barely) by a narcissistic mother who severely neglected me and my siblings. Mom spent most of her life chasing after a "Mr. Right" who would sweep her off her feet and rescue her from all the trials of everyday life. You gotta understand some basic truths about narcissists: the only person they care about is themselves. They are never wrong, they are justified in all their choices, and baby, it is always, ever *only* about *them*.

Mom was never around. She would go to work, doing whatever get-rich-quick scheme that others could fund. She was a master at starting (and closing down) businesses, and she worked nights in night clubs (or did she? I really don't know) looking for her knight in shining armor. I have no memory of spending time with my mother as a child. By the time I was nine years old, it was my job as the only girl at home to take care of the domestic details such as grocery shopping. Mom would sit in the car reading her Barbara Cartland romance novel and send me into the store with a list. I would then do the shopping and write the amount on the check. I was NINE!

Daisy, the cashier, was always so kind to me. She knew my mom was sitting in the car and she would help me with the check. I can remember her smiling at me as she showed me what to do, and I remember thinking it was weird that she had braces at her age. Looking back now, she was probably in her forties, but she seemed a lot older to me at the time.

We all had to do the laundry and sometimes Mom would call from work and tell me to put a chicken, or a pot roast, or box of Banquet frozen fried chicken in the oven and make a salad for my older brothers. I would do that or we would all just eat our favorite peanut butter and jelly with a glass of sugar-packed Kool-Aid. I learned how to cope (no, *survive*) at an early age.

Life was in a constant state of upheaval. My mom was married seven times: SEVEN, *siete*, 7 times—often to alcoholics. Of course, if you were to ask her, not once was the failure of the marriage her fault. Do you have any narcissists in your life? Narcissists believe that they are without fault and that they are always justified in their reasoning, choices, or actions. Whatever the problem was, Mom was always looking outside of herself to fix it. In her mind, the cure had to be external. She was always looking to make a quick buck, always angling for the next best deal.

Narcissists only care about you when you can do something for them. Mom wanted me around on Saturday morning to play nursemaid and make her cups of tea because she was "exhausted from such a tough week." If you spend much time around a person with this set of traits, you will quickly learn that they LOVE drama; they love attention of any kind, good or bad, and will stop at nothing to be sure they get it—they are addicted to their story. They LOVE their story.

A narcissist will almost never take responsibility for their actions. They will find a way to turn things around and make themselves the main focus. When I was starting Grade Six, Mom fell in love with an Iraqi pilot. His longest layovers were in Greece. So, guess what she decided? Yup, "We're moving to Greece." She bailed on my older brothers and literally left them behind in Seattle as she dragged me to Greece. She had an elaborate fantasy that everything would fall into place and she could home-school me while we lived in the Mediterranean. It wasn't long before, once again, I was taking care of her. I was shopping, cooking, and trying to learn the language. We returned to the United States after four and a half months with me never having opened a textbook.

My sister is ten years older than me, so once she was married and had her own place, Mom would often ship me off to live with her, more or less dumping us kids off on the eldest. Side note: I am very close with my siblings.

My father was an icon and respected in the community. I loved Dad dearly and looked forward to the time I spent with him. Dad made it clear that he cherished me; on his weekends, he would take me to lunch and introduce me to his friends. Valentine's Day was a major celebration in Dad's book: one year, he gave me a new bike; another time, it was a canopy bed. But we knew that we had to watch his moods and be careful after 5 p.m. because Dad was a functioning alcoholic. He was a mean drunk, and once he'd had too much, he was no fun to be around. Loving him and wanting to please him, I often found myself walking on eggshells for fear of disappointing him.

I made it my role in the family to be the peacemaker, willing to sacrifice my own happiness if it meant everyone would get along. At the age of 12, I got my first job cleaning the meat department at a local grocery store. By the time I was 14 years old, I was no longer living with a parent at all. I had moved out and was, more or less, spare space, a.k.a. crashing where I could, living with other families or friends, and at my Grandma's house on the other side of town (three buses from my school). I dropped out of high school in my junior year, got my General Equivalency Diploma, and went to college. But it wasn't for me. I realized that I would be earning the same amount of money per year after college with my degree that I was making working jobs already. Can you guess what I did? Absolutely! I dropped out of college after my second semester.

Eventually, I found my path and began to establish myself as an adult. I found a steady job and my own place. But I didn't realize how much of my past was still ingrained in my paradigms. Even though it looked like I was doing great, I had started down the same path as my mother. You are not going to believe this, but I ended up married to an abusive alcoholic.

Okay, time out. Let's press pause for a second. I'm not sitting here crying, "Poor little me." I am truly grateful for the lessons I have learned, even if they were shitty at the time. My experiences have brought me to where I am today, so I am grateful for them, good and bad (and I learned how to shop at the grocery store for a good value, right?).

I ended up divorcing the abusive, alcoholic guy at 26. But while I managed to get rid of him at the corner of dysfunction junction, he left me shackled to a mountain of debt that took years to finally sort out and pay. Around the same time, I lost my job when the company I worked for went bankrupt. All these things fueled my desire to become MORE. I realized that I had a choice. I hit a point where I either had to change or become my mother. (Oh, HELL to the NO!) Enough is enough.

> *The reason this book is in your hand is that, on some level, you've been thinking the same thing: something's gotta change.*

That thought lit a fire under my ass and truly propelled me to look at my life and my responsibilities. It would have been easy to be the victim. There was a long laundry list of shit he did: drinking, cheating, abuse, running up the credit cards, quitting jobs-- DUDE! I could point my finger at my ex-husband and the bad things he did to me, but I would have three fingers pointing back at myself, asking, "Sam, what the hell is wrong with you that you allowed him to treat you that way?" I had to own *all* my choices. When I asked myself, "How can you accept that?" I had my answer: no more. You can't change other people; you can only change YOU.

But here is the deal: if I learned anything from my Mom's lack of taking responsibility, it was that playing victim doesn't solve YOUR issue. The lesson Mom taught me through her years of searching was that *I am the only one who can take responsibility for my life*. I needed not to blame, but to change. I am not kidding. I literally asked myself these questions: *What is going on with you, Sam, that you would allow that treatment for so long? What can I do to fix me?* I started doing "The Work." I decided on a better life.

Within a few years, I worked my way back up the corporate ladder and earned myself a position that came with the prestige and paycheck that most people would feel pretty good about. Financial success equaled security to me. I had learned that I couldn't rely on anyone else for that security, not my parents, not my ex, just me. So, I made it my priority.

Over time, I realized that my job didn't fulfill me like it once did. Sure, it came with some sweet perks, but it meant working between two offices, one in Washington and one in Texas. I spent my life in a suitcase, traveling between the two states and living in hotels. I was a vice-president, responsible for employees nationwide. I had money and a big title, but I still wasn't really happy. Having a boyfriend in Seattle that I never saw and a beautiful condo that I hardly got to sleep in—where's the fun in that? Making cash at the expense of losing all your time sucks too. I had my financial security, but the price was all my fun. I was stuck in a rut and it was time to make a change. I had done it before, and it was time to do it again.

One Decision Can Make All the Difference

So, I quit my high paying job. I took my big, heavy, fifteen-pound Dell computer (this was, after all, the late 1990s), sat on the floor at the gate of the Dallas Fort Worth Airport, and made a simple list of things I wanted for my life. By writing it down, I was making it real. It was a declaration to God and the universe that I was fed up. I was ready to make the change.

Then, I started taking small steps toward those things. What blew my mind was that within twelve months I had everything on my list except the guy that I ended up with was not taller than me. (I'm 6'2". You gotta learn to be flexible!) That practice, that list, changed my life forever.

Now, my life is always about moving forward and as I learned to help myself, an amazing thing happened: I was able to help others too. I can truly say that I live a blessed life, including a wonderful husband who I have been happily married to for almost 20 years.

Are You Stuck?

As you will learn throughout this book, awareness is one of the key ingredients to not being stuck in life. But how do you know when you are stuck? I have met many people who thought that they were doing fine. As we worked together, they realized that they were indeed doing fine and sometimes even good, but not doing great. They were actually stuck: some a little stuck, some a lot stuck. Once that realization comes, that is when the real progress begins; that is when they are able to start seeing their dream life come true.

You know that your life needs to change in some way; otherwise, you wouldn't be reading this book. Like many others, though, you are not sure why you feel the way that you do, or how to stop feeling the way you do. If you find yourself feeling stuck, and you are ready to change, I am here to help you on your journey.

Signs That You Are Stuck

So, how can you tell when you are stuck in life? Let's look at some signals.

Confusion: The "I don't know" game

Is your life full of "I don't knows"? If someone asks you about your goals in life and you can't answer the question, or the answers you do give are very vague and generalized, that is a sign of confusion. Confusion keeps you stuck because it prevents you from making decisions for your life. You let circumstances and other people dictate what you are worthy of or what your life is going to look like, which leaves you stuck in someone else's plan.

My clients never get to say "I don't know" to me. They can, but I don't let it sit there. I always reply, "What if you did know, then what would it look like?" I ask them, "So, what would you love?" There is always something that someone loves. I start by helping them to see the big picture of things that they would love in life and, over time, we narrow it down to the life they would love to live and then to act on those things.

Lack of Motivation

Does this sound like you? "I don't want to do this today. I don't want to get out of bed. I'm just not interested in going to work. I'm not interested in making dinner. I'm not interested. I just don't feel like it." When you are stuck, nothing really seems appealing because you are not being motivated by any positive or fulfilling future. Why bother to do anything when nothing is going to change anyway?

Depression

This can range from a mild funk to severe depression. If you feel that it is mild and short term, then you will find that getting unstuck will push it out of the driver's seat. If you feel that it is more severe or it has lasted for a long time (two weeks or longer), then you need to seek professional help. Making good choices in life will always help you get unstuck, even when that means getting medical support to move you forward.

Anxiety

This is a big one. Are you worried about what might, possibly, maybe, happen? Do you ask or think to yourself, "What if [insert undesirable or negative thought here]?" a lot? Do you feel like you are so concerned about the future that you can't live in the now? Anxiety is something that traps you in its hold. Your life can become centered around it or it can consume you. And, yes, it is a horrible place to be. I know, I have been there. Sometimes, I find myself dipping my toe in the anxiety pond even today. Thankfully, you can break free from its grasp, and this book will help you to learn how you can live in confidence instead of fear.

Complacency

Complacency, to me, is like the color beige. I mean, it's alright, but it doesn't fire me up. It is a blah type of life where you just settle for whatever comes your way. You use words like, "I'm fine, I'm okay." Sometimes I feel like I want to kick people in the ass when they are in that complacent state and say to them, "You're not fine; you're stuck. You are settling for a life so beneath what you are worthy of and you don't even know it. There is so much available to you in life right now!" Okay, sometimes I DO, actually do that to my clients!

Complacency can also keep you from reaching out for help. You keep yourself apart from others because you don't want to be a burden to them or be judged. It is not fun and is a small way to live.

When I coach complacent people, it can be hard to get them to see that they are stuck because "everything is fine" (beige). This isn't really true, as often people come to coaching because, deep down, they know they are stuck. At the opposite end of the pendulum are people who think I am a therapist and want me to energize their story. They say to me, "You have to hear what happened TO me." They are addicted to their past, their story and therefore stay stuck. Living in the past is a sure-fire way to stay stuck. I coach people to live in THE NOW, to dream up lives they would love to live, and then do just that! Now, also known as the present, is all we really have.

Tired/Lazy

There are two things that can be the cause of tiredness and laziness. One is medical reasons. Maybe there is something going on with you physically and there is a totally valid reason why you feel that way.

The other is that you are stuck and that is your excuse for it. There is a physical law that states that objects at rest want to stay at rest. Objects in motion want to keep moving, and it takes a lot of energy to change either state.

The longer you have been stuck, the more tired and lazy you will feel. Now, whether you're tired because of medical reasons or because you are stuck, it doesn't matter. If you want things to change, then you need to address what is going on and take action. It will get better if you do; I know this for sure.

One of the things I experienced in my perimenopausal state is anemia or low blood levels. It makes you very tired. When this started to happen, I was napping two hours a day. But that wasn't the solution, and I had a decision to make: give into it and use it as an excuse (which I see many people do and I did for a while as well), or deal with it and get back to the life I love living. Can you guess what I decided to do? Of course, I hit it head-on. I changed a lot. Now, I eat foods that are good for my body; I take supplements to increase my levels; I make sure that I sleep enough, but not too much; and I keep in motion (with the occasional nap, of course, as a treat).

There is a difference between fact and truth. "I'm so tired. I have no motivation. I can't keep my eyes open, and I just want to take a two-hour nap." That's a fact. That's how you feel. So, you can sit there and say, "I'm so tired because I'm anemic. I'm so tired because of my hormones. I'm so tired because of my thyroid," and you will stay stuck in that place.

The truth is that there is something you can do about it. You can seek medical advice. You can eat better and exercise to build up strength. You can get yourself into a proper sleep cycle. You can take supplements. You can get rid of some of the stress in your life that may be causing the condition in the first place. That is the truth.

Wishing for More, but Not Taking Action

You can tell this is you if you live in the land of "I would, BUT." "I would do this, but…" "This seems like a great idea, but…" There is always some great excuse such as, "I don't have the education, I live in the wrong area, I am a woman, I am too old, I'm too this, I'm too that."

You let conditions and circumstances rule you and they become an invisible wall that keeps you stuck.

If you are waiting for the conditions or circumstances to change and then you will take some action, or if you find yourself saying, "I will do it when XYZ happens," then I am here to ring your bell. It doesn't work that way. You must take action first and then the conditions and circumstances will universally move around you. Again, trust me on this.

I spent a large part of my career in sales and sales training. Customers would often say, "I need to research and analyze this before I can make a decision." That is another way of saying, "I will analyze this to death and most likely never make a decision."

I saw it happening over and over and over again. There is an old saying: "He who needs all the information to make a decision never makes a decision." They get stuck.

The other words you use are, "I don't know how." When I do workshops with my clients, one of the first things I do is have them write the word HOW on their notebook, and then I have them draw a line through it to cross it out and replace "how" by writing "what." The *how* is none of their business. I tell them, "If you want to get stuck, try and figure out the how." If you want to love your life, ask yourself WHAT can I do? What is one thing I can do, big or small, to start the process? There is always something you can do.

Fear

Fear of failure, fear of success, fear of what people will think, and fear of being found out can paralyze you. What if I put myself out there and they see me for who I really am and judge me? This includes the "I am not enough" talk and the "What if" talk. Fear will always keep you stuck, and the longer you stay in it, the more of a grip it has on you, the more it becomes a habit. When you move away from being paralyzed with fear when you are in the practice of leaning in, then staying out of the stuck zone becomes easier and easier.

Addiction to Your Story

Finally, so many people are stuck because they are addicted to their story. I mentioned this a bit earlier when talking about complacency. You are so used to being stuck in the past and use your "story" as a way to stay stuck, to have an excuse to not move into the amazing life waiting for you. I hear this often in phrases like, "You don't know what happened to me, Sam."

Some clients come into my office and they love to tell me how they want to change, but they feel like they have to tell me their whole life story first. In integrity, I tell them, "It's your money, but I don't need to know what happened to you. I am much more interested in what you want to make happen in your life, but if you feel it's really important, then you can tell me your story."

I'm not interested in what happened to you only because you think I should feel sorry for you or give you some sort of a pass. What I am interested in is where you are going! If you want a professional to commiserate with you about your past, then you should go see a therapist. They are awesome at listening to your stories and are wonderful and instrumental in helping you make peace with your past. But that is not where I, as a coach, live. I don't see the growth in the "I do this, or behave this way, because this happened to me" kind of thinking. Um… but we are leaving your old story behind so you can get unstuck. When you live in the past, you stay stuck. If you'd like to stop feeling stuck, then you are going to work with me and we are going to go forward and create new thinking habits and new truths. The past was a gift; it was a place to learn and move on from.

We are going to let go of the "What happened to me" story. We are going to change those paradigms and move you into designing a life you love.

I shared my story with you because, first of all, you need to know that I have lived what I teach. I am not some guru who just studied to become a coach and write a book. I am you, a real person who has had many struggles and decided to change. The truth is I actually hate telling my story and I left out a lot of the ugly details because, honestly, I left that stress, anxiety, and struggle a long time ago. I simply don't live there anymore.

I also didn't tell you my story to impress you; I told you to impress *upon you* that we all have a story, but we are not, repeat, ARE NOT our story. We all have a past, but we are not our past. I know that what is within us is so much greater than any circumstance outside of us, and it is time to become more than even we had imagined.

Okay, You Got Me, I'm Stuck. Now What?

I will give you a quick and effective tip right here, right now. Let go and leave your old stories, your past fears, anger, pain, and dramas behind. I am not telling you to deny them; I am telling you to deny the energy you give to them. You cannot move forward if you are carrying a bunch of old crap. If you decide to let go and do the lifework that I prescribe in the following chapters, then you too will live a purposefully "Designed life."

I am not one to beat around the bush. Being stuck sucks! I wrote the title of this book to tell you exactly what it is about. It's for those people who actually want to get UN-stuck, Unsucked, or Un*ucked. As weird as that might sound, a lot of people I have met through the years in my coaching practice want to stay in their story. They secretly (or not so secretly) are comfortable in their drama and their "I can't because…" thinking. This book is not about feeding, energizing, or trying to impress yourself or anyone else with those old stories, patterns, or paradigms. Give them up! Clearly, they are not working for you anymore.

You are not going to be fixed just because you read this book either. What you can expect by following the steps and doing the lifework is becoming freer and getting a real taste of the life that is waiting for you, a life that you can and will really love.

Think of these practices like a recipe. For this example, let's make cookies. (Who doesn't love cookies?) Each ingredient on its own may not taste very good. Sugar? Yum! Chocolate? Yum! Raw eggs? Not so much. Pure vanilla extract? Pretty intense. However, when all the ingredients are mixed together, then they become a delicious harmonious blend and take form to become wonderful, delicious cookies.

Now, let's say you leave out an ingredient because you don't like how it tastes on its own. You decide to leave out the raw eggs. What happens? You get flat, dry, biscuit-like things that fall apart. This is not what you wanted to create, is it? Didn't you decide to make something delicious and wonderful?

If someone said, "What happened to your cookies?" You wouldn't say, "I don't know, the recipe must not work," would you? No, you would say, "I thought I could make it without the eggs; lesson learned. I will add together all the ingredients next time as I know, now, it is necessary to get me my delicious cookies." Maybe you wouldn't use those exact words, but you get the gist! Use all the steps like you would use all the ingredients in a proven recipe.

Have faith, trust, and follow the steps. Put your pen to paper and reap the rewards. These practices work; they are the ingredients that on their own sometimes taste good and sometimes are hard to stomach, but when mixed together, they will create harmony. Harmony in your life! Something delicious. Here's to you, designing your life. Happy baking!

Chapter 2
GRAND OVERALL DESIGNER

> *There are only two ways to live your life: one is though nothing is a miracle. The other is though everything is a miracle.*
> **Albert Einstein**

Some of you reading this book may see the places where I talk about G.O.D. and feel a little cringe. You might think, "Nuh-uh. That's woo-woo talk." That's okay. I am not trying to convert you to anything or sign you up for the First Superchurch of Sam.

My goal is to be inclusionary. I am offering my personal experiences and the lessons I have received in my life. I believe that there is something bigger than you and me, something bigger than all of us. My name for this higher power is the Grand Overall Designer, or G.O.D., for short.

I did a little research this morning. I was wondering how many religions there were in the United States. After a quick Google search, I found some unbelievable statistics. The phrase "one nation under God" can mean something different to members of approximately 313 religions and dominations in the United States alone. Crazy, right?

That covers a lot of bases. It could be the God that Judeo-Christian and other traditions follow, or the belief in many Gods, or those who believe in no God, or a God that is represented by animal spirits or alien groups, or psychoactive substances. The reason that I don't talk about a specific "God" is that I don't want to exclude people from the growth or from the power that is greater than us. I want to offer you the opportunity to consider a non-exclusionary definition of G.O.D. that will fit in your world view.

Unfortunately, we live in a world where people are very judgmental. I ask clients about their spiritual life in their initial strategy session when we are first considering working together and interviewing each other. When I ask them about what they believe, I can't tell you how many people respond, "I'm spiritual, but I'm not religious."

It's amazing how many people will jump to "I'm not religious." They are anxious to reassure me about that. Often, they are not quite sure what they believe in, but they believe in something greater than themselves.

Then again, I have clients that are Jewish, Greek Orthodox, Catholic, and other varieties of Christian. I also have clients that are agnostic, non-denominational, and atheists. But a majority of them are much more comfortable outside of the confines of a traditional (or strict) religion because they are more at ease in the belief that something out there is bigger than them. They just don't want to be categorized into having to say, believe, or act in a certain way. When that happens, belief systems become restrictive and stifling. They are not free-flowing.

The brilliant theoretical physicist Steven Hawking wrote a book called *The Grand Design*, which talks about the measure of total energy in the universe. As an avowed atheist, he believed in the laws of science. So, that could be the power that is greater than us as well, which is why I say, Grand Overall Designer. What falls underneath that large umbrella term? What is the Grand Overall Designer? What is it to you? I'm not here to tell somebody what that is for them.

I'm not here to tell you what you believe in or try to convince you to believe in a certain thing. I am going to tell you that if you are an atheist and you only believe in science, then, well, you know, one of our greatest minds in science was Steven Hawking, and he talks about the world being energy. Maybe you won't hand over your thoughts or your problems to a God, but consider allowing that there is a power greater than you to help you out.

Everything has a vibration. From an ocean wave to a guitar string to our own heartbeat, all objects have a frequency at which they will vibrate. Even our thoughts vibrate. Our thoughts and physical things have different frequencies. If we can agree that thoughts are things with a vibration and energy, then these vibrations could be your message to G.O.D., to *your* Grand Overall Designer, or it could be how the universe is responding to your vibration.

That's what is really cool about the Grand Overall Designer concept. I am not pitching any one idea. There's something we all agree on: there is something out there that is bigger than us. Even the scientists will tell you that—it's called the universe. And the universe is responding and acting in a certain way. Cool, huh?

I was raised in a Unity Church. I was also introduced to New Age thinking by my mother, who was extremely interested in metaphysics and New Age ideas. She would often take me to different groups to try whatever "flavor of the month" she was following at that time. Don't get me wrong, not all of it was cray-cray. Some of it has been very useful in my life and has helped me help others for a long time. My grandmother was also a member of the Unity Church. She often took me to church on Sundays and could quote lots of verses from the Bible. My grandma ROCKED!

As an adult, when things got really rough for me, that would be the place I would go to for inspiration. My experience with the Unity Church was that it's non-judgmental. It uses both the Bible and *A Course in Miracles* (sometimes referred to as ACIM).

I attended a church with my friend's parents when I was a kid, but I walked out on the day I was told if I didn't attend *that denomination,* I would burn in hell. Obviously, since my whole family was not in church that day, I turned and ran from such a hard-line message that seemed to have no room for forgiveness.

I had a conversation with my boyfriend (now my husband) back when we were just dating; he was trying to convince me that he was an atheist. I remember saying, that's kind of a problem for me because how do you not have faith in at least *something*? Where does faith come from, then? I told him that if you think that this is just you on your own, by yourself, and with nothing else out there,—I told him, then your life must have been pretty damn easy if you never had to dig deep for faith.

I think the Grand Overall Designer needs to be present because when we hit potholes, when we hit problems, we have to dig in and know that there is something greater out there for us. We are not in this alone. That's how I came to know God: through my grandmother and my mom. And then that faith became one of the places that gave me comfort. As I got older, I would go by myself to search out that peace.

There's a line I heard about five or six years ago in a seminar: a good message is a good message *regardless of the source.* When I am working with groups, I use it every time. Please don't shut down when you see or hear phrases like, "Oh, it's a God thing", or "It's a religion thing", or "It's a metaphysical woo-woo thing, an astrology thing." It is all of these things and none of these things!

Like the Golden Rule says: do unto others as you would have them do to you. Buddhists believe that, Christians believe that—most people believe that. It often boils down to "Don't be a jerk." Be nice to people. Be kind. It's amazing when you start looking at those values, let's just call them beliefs, held by the different religions. You are going to find that Muslims, Christians, and Buddhists share certain core values that are almost identical.

In other words, listen for what rings true to determine whether the message is true for you. Be open to the idea, regardless of the source. Don't pass judgment because it came from a Buddhist monk, or cross your arms and shake your head because it didn't come from the Bible (or from Wittgenstein, for that matter). I'm asking you to take the source out of the equation and ask: Is it a good message? Is it useful? Will it serve you? Take the time to chew on the thought a bit and ask yourself, what's in this message for me? Tell me what you mean by that.

You may have begun this chapter feeling somewhat neutral to slightly antagonistic towards the concept of believing in something bigger than yourself. You may be asking, why do I benefit from believing anything? Because you are not alone. There is a force out there that you can tap into. There's something bigger than you that can support and match you. When you recognize that there is a power bigger than yourself that wants you to know it is aligned with you, then amazing things begin to happen.

Some people find it difficult to believe. They believe that there's nothing more than what we can perceive in the physical realm. They believe that when they die, everything stops, just like a candle that's been blown out. An empty shell will go into the ground and that's it. That's certainly one angle.

Let me pretend I am that person, saying, "Listen, I don't care what you do with my body when I'm gone. When I'm dead, it's over. There is no afterlife, there is no spirit, no soul; I'm done." Okay. That stance could be right, and after you are dead, none of this shit is going to matter.

That person would be on the scientific side of things, and you can't deny science. Laws are laws. Laws of gravity, attraction, and polarity are immutable and inescapable. However, I want to point out that this is a philosophical position as well. What if science and faith can coexist together in harmony? If you can't see the possibility that there is something greater than yourself or science *as we know it*, then you should probably burn this book, or recycle it or donate it to somebody that does believe.

There are certain shared values among most of the major religions on the planet, from Buddhism to Zoroastrianism. Truth, justice, peace within yourself and with others, and kindness. These are all examples of the commonalities of some very, very diverse thinking.

People are going to hold very strongly to their personal belief systems, but if we can understand that there are multitudes of people that believe and cherish things like honesty, compassion, and peace, perhaps then we can be united in working together for a common good. (Even if some people use different labels than we do.)

You may not subscribe to a particular religion of your own, but I am willing to bet that you share many of those values mentioned above. When you drill into so many of these different beliefs, the basis of them is rooted in kindness, loving, and taking care of each other. We are born with the ability to love, and a desire to share that love with other people.

Faith

What role does faith play in living successfully? Let me ask you this: what's your other choice? Fear? No thanks. When you are using your faith in your choices, you are hoping for the best and expecting the best. A sprinter laces their shoes, sets their toe in the block, and launches themselves down the track when the starter's pistol fires. There is no time wasted in fearing the outcome of the race. When a baby is learning to walk, her first steps are away from Mom and into the world. There may be dangerous things down the road, but that doesn't stop her from trying to explore.

Faith is something that pulls you and pushes you. It is energy. It's just as strong as the fear energy—they are two sides of the same coin. Faith gives you hope. Faith gives you belief. Faith gives you knowing. You have faith; tap into it. Just build it by trusting. It's already in there.

I remember having a conversation with my friend, Brad. He had been drifting for a while and he was discouraged. When I asked him how it was going, he said, "Yeah, my life sucks, as usual." I pointed out that he had had three job interviews that week, one of which seemed like an especially good fit. But Brad was on a roll. "The universe just wants to rip my head off and crap down my neck." (I know, gross statement, but that's what he said.) That became his mantra. He would get a job, but it wouldn't be long before he would be talking about what a bad place it was and, after a while, he was looking for work again. It got to the point where I had to limit the time I spent with Brad for my own mental health.

I realized that some people get so good at complaining that they instinctively try to keep the good away from them. They turn into somebody who would rather miss out than be proven wrong. All their faith has been channeled in the wrong direction.

The Universe, Spirit, and G.O.D. were responding to Brad. He had gotten so fixated on the energy of "I'm a victim here", that the Universe was saying, "Okay, you're a victim. You are getting screwed over. Let's give you more of *that*, if that's really what you want."

In his case, it wasn't what he wanted, but it *was* what he was tuned to. Dude, you are tuned to FOX News! Change the frequency a little bit and get to the Discovery Channel. It's a frequency shift. Otherwise, you are stuck on one channel. You are tuned into the channel of drama, the victim channel. You are tuned into endless drama, 24 hours a day, starring *you!*

Change the channel, change your frequency! What would you really like to be watching? What would you *really* like it to look like? If you would really like it to look like the Discovery Channel, or like HGTV, then start giving energy to those things and stop being stuck on FOX.

I trust everything will turn out for good because I believe we ultimately live in a place that was designed for our greater good. We probably all agree that the world is generally a good and favorable place to live. Most people would agree it's better to be alive than dead. We might be struggling in our own individual cases, but generally speaking, the planet is designed to be healthy. We might muck it up with pollution or fossil fuels, but there are fish in the sea, there's fertile land, and there's generally a world that was designed for our greater good.

We were designed to exist perfectly on this planet. We were actually given everything to not fail. Everything was put here, however it got here, perfectly. So, then, if we go back and ask, how can I trust that everything is going to turn out for good? It's because I have evidence of it in the natural world.

It goes back to our perception of things. We can sit there and say, "I want to be stuck in my problem and this bad thing that happened to me and there's no good in that." Well, that's your perception. That exact same experience can happen to somebody else and their perception will let them grow and look at all the good that came from the experience.

Think about those wicked wildfires that burned through British Columbia and California. You saw nightly interviews of people in shock, saying things like, "Oh my God, I lost everything." They were absolutely devastated and some likely thought, "How can this happen to me?" And then you had someone else in the same situation who said, "You know what, thankfully we weren't in the house. That's replaceable and we have our lives."

Your perception will either keep you stuck or set you free. There is a gift in every situation—if you look for it. The story of how one family lost everything can be a gift, years down the road, teaching them to be ready for things like the need to prepare and evacuate. There's a gift in everything; you have to look for it, and you have to decide how you want to feel and how you want to live. Everything can be put to use for our greater good. It's how we decide to use it.

You have to stretch your hand out and put the effort into using the lesson you were given. You can't just sit there like a baby bird waiting for the Universe, Spirit, or G.O.D. to go "bleah" and regurgitate it into your mouth. People say, "I prayed for it. I prayed for it", but did you believe that it would happen? How did you engage? Did you take any action, or did you just sit in a corner waiting? You can't sit there, lock yourself in a closet, and cross your fingers because you made a prayer. It takes belief and it takes action on your part.

Most prominent religions teach that we were created in the perfect image of God. Is this not true? Is this something you have heard before? Doesn't that mean you have all of the capabilities in the world?

Looking again at our planet: everything was created perfectly for us to thrive and to have beautiful, great, and awesome lives. Whether you believe that it was put here magically by God, or if the Universe created itself, it's pretty incredible.

Whatever you believe as to *how* it came about, we can agree that it was *designed* perfectly as a living ecosystem. Can you believe that there is a force still out there in your corner that is rooting for you? Can you tap into that? Energetically get into a match with it.

At a certain point, it takes more effort and more stubbornness to say, "No, I'm the only single person that this won't possibly work for."

This is a tough one because I don't want to exclude people. I have a very strong belief system in this. Then again, I am happily married to someone who thinks he is an atheist.

I say that my husband only *thinks* he is an atheist because sometimes when things don't happen in his favor, he will say, "I am a good person. Why did that happen to me?" I shake my head and think, *you are acting like there is something bigger than you out there that's dictating this. Who are you talking to? 'Cuz you always tell* me *it's a bunch of woo-woo.*

Decide in part what it is you want to believe in. Decide in part, you don't have to commit to any one thing right now. If you want to believe that it's you, that you are the only one, then put the book down—we're done. None of the principles I'm going to talk about will work with this attitude. I don't know a single person who truly believes in absolutely nothing. You can't believe there's not a universe and energy because, otherwise, you wouldn't be sitting; you would be floating around the room. Your body is giving you sensory evidence and your interaction with the world around you provides empirical evidence all the time.

So, we just peel it back. Peel back a corner of your mind. It's possible. It's possible that there's something bigger, better, and brighter than what you are experiencing now. Here's my one rule: you don't get to not have a perspective. There are no neutral parties here. It could be a small faith perspective, that's okay, but you don't get to say that you don't have one.

Chapter 3
FLUID THINKING

> *Live life to the fullest. You have to color outside the lines once in a while if you want to make your life a masterpiece. Laugh some every day. Keep growing, keep dreaming, keep following your heart. The important thing is not to stop questioning.*
> **Albert Einstein**

Conditions and Circumstances

I recently did a workshop where I was recalling my experience of going through the steps I instruct. I watch people as I teach them how to figure out what they love. Their faces have a mix of emotions—they want to believe it's possible, but they have doubts.

When I say to them, "What do you love?" They typically say, "I don't know," which, as we learned earlier, is one of the reasons why we stay stuck. "I don't know" or "I am confused" is our way of staying stuck.

I often give people my version of an assignment that my mentor Mary Morrisey taught me. First, I teach them the difference between what they would like and what they would love. I call the assignment, "Loves and Not Its." I tell them, let's dream up a life you would love, without conditions and circumstances, without the "I would love to do that, but…"

People tend to play a small game, saying, "Well, that will be great, but…" or "You know, I'd love to go and live in another country, but…" or "You know, I'd love to have a big house, but…" or "I'd love to change careers, but…" and so on.

The word "but" signals the conditions and circumstances that prevent people from living the life they love. For example, they say things like, "But I don't have the education", "But I don't know how", "But I don't speak the language."

Do you see what I'm saying? We can call them excuses, but I prefer to explain them as conditions and circumstances. "Because of these conditions, I can't do *x*.". Or, "Because of these circumstances, I can't do *y*." This is absolutely untrue; you are capable of anything your mind conceives—you are putting these limits on yourself.

Let's Get Started

"You will Actually will need to go to www.Adesignedlifellc.com and print your workbook." First, you will need a blank notebook and a pen. I have actually made life really easy for you by creating the notebook/study guide for you. Go to www.aDesignedLifellc.com and look for your UNS*UCK workbook and print. You are going to write in an actual notebook to get the full benefit of this exercise. Even if you have an editing feature on your e-reader, take the extra time to write it out by hand. Don't tell me you have lousy handwriting, or you prefer to do it on your computer. You need to WRITE and DO THE EXERCISES for the change you are craving to take place. Reading this stuff will help you know *about it*, but physically doing the exercises will help you *know it*! There is a big difference between the two, trust me.

Dream It Up

When Mary Morrissey starts this exercise, she asks: "What would you love?"

I will ask you the same thing. What would you love? What would you love to have, what would you love to be, and what would you love to feel? Let's just say we are dreaming and you could have it all, without restrictions or conditions. You could have everything you love, without waiting for a change in circumstances, and regardless of where you are right now or what you have experienced so far in your life. What would you love that would give you a spark? What would give you a charge, security, or excitement? It is time to start dreaming again. Get rid of the "I can't because" and "I would, but" thinking, and you absolutely cannot say, "I don't know." Remember, you want to ACTUALLY get UN-stuck, Un-Sucked, Un*ucked.

So, don't play the "I don't know" game. You do know. At some level or possibly many levels, you do know. Saying "I don't know" or "I'm confused" is the part of you that is trying to stay stuck. Knock it off. You got this.

Exercise #1

Get your notebook and draw a line down the center of a page from top to bottom. Title the top left "LOVE", and on the other side of the line, write "NOT IT". Now, I want you to think (or dream up) what you would LOVE in your life. And, almost guaranteed, your mind will soon come up with all the things that are NOT IT, the things that you don't love.

Ask yourself: What are the four most important areas of your life where you would like to see change? Pick four from the list below to get started:

- Physical Health
- Mental Well-being
- Relationships
- Love
- Time Freedom
- Money Freedom
- Fun/Leisure
- Giving/Philanthropy
- Spirituality
- Career
- Creativity

This should take several pages of your notebook, so leave enough room to write everything down.

Ask yourself: What would I love to be? What would I love to feel? What would I love to have or experience? What would I LOVE in the area of _____ *(look at your choices above)*

Start writing your answers to these questions in your notebook. Don't try to ignore the NOT IT section; just write them on the right side of your list and keep going on your LOVEs. When you feel you have described enough LOVEs in one life area, it is time to move to the next area. Keep asking yourself, "What would I LOVE?" in every one of the four areas of your life, until you have completed all four.

In this first exercise, I will ask you to let go of your conditions and circumstances. Put these limitations to one side and give yourself permission to dream.

LOVE	NOT IT

You can find a full-page version of this exercise at the end of the book. Here are some ideas or examples of LOVEs and how you could get more specific in each of the categories:

- **Career and Creative Expression.** "Work I would love to do" and/or "Ways I want to use my special hobbies or gifts."

- **Health and Well-being.** This includes physical, spiritual, and mental health. "I would love to be lean, strong, and healthy." "I would love to be working with a life coach and going to church regularly."

- **Time, Money, and Freedom.** "I'd love to travel and vacation six weeks a year." "My house is paid for and I have more than enough money to give in areas and ways that I want to give."

- **Love and Relationships.** "My partner and I are fun, loving and super-communicators.", "I have a few close friends that I know I can count on. I could call them at 3 am and they would help me." "I have a great relationship with my children. We are close, affectionate and I can see my children building compassionate, thoughtful relationships with their friends. They are confident to stand up against peer pressure and behave with integrity."

Here is an example of a completed list:

LOVE		NOT IT
I love creating online content for websites and blog posts.		Writing boring ad copy.
I would love to create videos where I get to interview musicians.		Studying for hours on end.
Working from home.		Commuting 1½ hours every day.
Vacations three times a year.		Putting off my vacation—again!

Now that your LOVE and NOT IT sections are filled, you will want to go back to your NOT ITs and reframe them to LOVEs. This is how to do it: if you know you don't want to write boring ad copy, what would you love instead? (Add the answer to the LOVE side.) For example, I love being creative and my writing skills are utilized when I am doing work that I love.

If you know you do not want to commute one-and-a-half hours daily to work and back, what would you love? (Again, add the answer to the LOVE side.) If a NOT IT is putting off vacation, then "I take regular vacations" could be the LOVE, right? As you reframe the NOT IT list and rewrite it in the opposite column, cross each item them off the NOT IT side. That was the old way of thinking.

Let's show them here what the new list looks like.

LOVE	NOT IT
I love creating online content for websites and blog posts.	~~Writing boring ad copy.~~
I would love to create videos interviewing musicians.	~~studying for hours on end.~~
Working from home.	~~Commuting 1½ hours every day.~~
Vacations three times a year.	~~Putting off my vacation again!~~
I love being creative and my writing skills are utilized when I am doing work that I love.	
I take Regular vacations	
I learn things easily and in a short amount of time. I am proficient	

Sandra's Story

Sandra was a client who was considering a career change. She was a successful realtor, but she wasn't really feeling fulfilled. So, I walked her through this exercise. We started with creating a "What would I love" list. I asked her, "Sandra, what would *you* love?" (Sometimes, the question is what *DO* you love because you may not be stuck in all areas of your life.)

"I really love design," she began. "I love fabrics and cool pieces of furniture, but not just decorating." We dug in a little deeper and I asked Sandra more questions about what she loved. She began to describe how she loved those design shows on TV where they go in and move walls, create cool spaces, and transform rooms.

"Let me understand. You love not only the decorating of a space but actually designing it—the structure and renovation?" I clarified.

"YES! Yes, that's it!" she said. Then, just as quickly, she blurted out, "But I don't want to work with bitchy clients." I laughed. I get it. No bitchy clients!

"RIGHT, no bitchy clients! Sandra then wrote "No bitchy clients" on the NOT IT side of the page. On the left side of the paper, under LOVE, Sandra wrote: design, cool pieces of furniture, fabrics, and moving walls. We talked more and listed other things that she loves, like taking an entire month off to travel during the summer, and lots of three-day weekends throughout the year.

Once we felt that we had plenty of LOVEs to begin forming a clear image in her mind, we went to work on the NOT IT side of the paper. We looked at where Sandra had immediately written under the NOT IT side, the stuff that she knew she didn't want that had popped into her head. We reframed those NOT ITs into LOVEs by creating positive statements. For example, we reframed (or rephrased) the negative statement, "I don't want to work with bitchy clients" to become the positive statement, "I work with easy and amazing clients who love my ideas."

Exercise: Write Out Your Future

Now that you have created your list of LOVEs, it's time to put them to work for you! On a fresh page, begin writing about what your life will look like in one, two, or three years in the future. Think about what your daily life would be like when you love everything in it. Think about the people you have in your life, and how those relationships add richness to your experience. Think about the little details to make your mental picture as clear as a photograph or a movie. This is your new story, the script for the life that you will design.

Let's lay out the most common area of people's lives to develop here again:

- **Career and creative expression**
- **Health and well-being**
- **Time freedom, money freedom**
- **Love and relationships**

My friend Diane was working on this LOVE/NOT IT exercise the other day. "What I would really love is having this full staff of absolutely self-driven, self-managed team players. That would allow me to focus on the projects that I really love, and let me do a lot of sales, and interacting with clients," she said.

Just like Diane, you're *living your story* right now. Imagine your life is in a giant book. You will see the chapters behind you and the ones yet to be written. Don't you want it to be an awesome read? We're going to tell this new story as if you already have it. So, we'll say it as if it was a prayer of gratitude. In Diane's case, it went, "I am so happy and grateful that I have an amazing staff. They are so fantastic. They are team players; they create such a positive environment for my clients." Whatever you would love to see manifested in your life, you will act as if you already have it.

Vision Exercise: Crafting the Life You LOVE

Okay, now writing and describing the things that you LOVE in your notebook has planted the seed, but just like a garden, you have to tend your vision. Read your script every day to make it part of your daily life. The entire vision has to be nurtured to manifest in your life. Take your time and think about this over a few days to really crystallize your vision. You may find there are areas in your script that will change as you grow and want different things. That's okay, that's why you need to keep coming back and reading your vision daily, to make sure it's still the life you LOVE.

We made a list of Diane's LOVEs: autonomy, benefits, amazing insurance for her and her team, working with good people, co-workers who are supporters, mentors. Then, suddenly, negatives started to pop into the story. Diane started to slow down and look heavy. "I don't want to travel like I used to do for work. Oh! That sounds negative," she said. "I better not think that. I better cancel that thought, right?"

"Go ahead and write it down. We can use it," I said. "Really? I figured that kind of negative thinking wasn't allowed," she replied.

Were you ever raised to say "cancel that thought" if it was negative? I personally don't believe that trick works. And here's why: if I said to you, "Think about Paris. Picture it in your mind." What is the main image that comes to your mind when I say picture Paris? Of course, it would be the beautiful Eiffel Tower, with its twinkling lights, its four legs, and lace-like structure, standing alone in the distance. You can see it in your mind, right?

Okay. Wait, wait, wait. *Cancel that thought.* Don't see the Eiffel Tower, with its twinkling lights, its four legs, and lace-like structure, standing alone in the distance. Whatever you do right now, don't picture the Eiffel Tower. Of course, you are still picturing the Eiffel Tower in your mind right now. True?

So, if you insist on getting all-powerful with "cancel that thought," then guess what? You just give more energy to the thought. We don't cancel thoughts. We *reframe* them. We don't ignore them; we replace them.

Let's take Diane's statement again, "I don't want to travel for business like I do now." Perfect, but what *do* you want? That's the key. You already know that you don't want to travel so much. What do you want? "I want to travel a couple of days a month," was the reply. Excellent. In the job you love, you have the autonomy, benefits and amazing insurance, co-workers who are really good people, and you only travel a couple of days a month. That's how you figure out what you love, and how you get rid of what you don't—you reframe the thought.

There is a flip side of NOT IT. You don't give the energy to the NOT IT stuff. You say, "Okay if I don't want that, what's the flip side of it? What's the replacement that I would love?"

Maybe this is a new idea for you. There are a lot of people who don't think it's possible to live a life you love. Perhaps you have been in negative patterns for so long that you can't even imagine these possibilities I am describing are available to you. But I can tell you with complete certainty that living a life you love *is* possible for *you*.

But there's a catch.

Aha! I knew it, you think. *Here it comes.*

Here's the catch: as long as you don't think it's possible for you to live a life you love, that will be your reality.

I know it seems like a reach right now, but if you can peel back the corner of your mind and just believe that a piece of it is possible, then we can start. And as that possibility starts being created and manifested, as it shows up and is built upon, you will have your proof. Then you will say, "Holy crap. This stuff works! It's happening—it's working!" And then, even more becomes possible for you.

But you have to get past your conditions and circumstances, kick your limiting beliefs out of the driver's seat of your life, and stop putting energy into thinking how stuck you are. Stop energizing how you are stuck in your job, or you're stuck in your house, or you're stuck in your neighborhood, or in your city, or in life. Stop. Ask yourself: what would I really love in this situation? What is a thing I could do today to move in the direction of having that?

Now I'll ask you the same question: is living a life you love possible? Yes, absolutely, *if you believe it is possible.* As Napoleon Hill famously said, "Whatever the mind can conceive and believe, the mind can achieve regardless of how many times you may have failed in the past or how lofty your aims and hopes may be."

I've worked with many, many people who wanted change in their lives, who wanted to get unstuck. They were stuck in the question of "How do I do it?" Or sometimes they ask, "What if I don't believe it is possible?"

Okay, I get it, I understand. Let me ask you: what *can* you believe? Let's just start with what you can believe. What can you get behind? Do you believe it's possible to be at your ideal weight? Great. Do you believe it's possible to work less than 40 hours a week and enjoy time with your family? Yes. Do you believe it's possible to learn a new craft or skill? Yes. Okay, so there we go. This is where we start.

Everything that I do with this fluid thinking is reverse engineering. Fluid thinking is the intentional rewiring of old, negative thought patterns with new, positive thoughts that will allow you to break free of that unstuck place. First, you must create the vision. What would you love? Then, we write a story as if we already have it, as described earlier in the "Write Out Your Future" exercise. Our new story is our direct message to G.O.D., the Grand Overall Designer (which you may know as Spirit,

Universal Intelligence, or Source), saying, "I love having this in my life." You are tricking your subconscious as you read your story about already having all this greatness. You trick your subconscious mind. Your subconscious mind is thinking, "I'm so dumb, I just believe whatever you tell me." It sits there and says, "Cool, I have total autonomy at work. I do work with good people. I do have a great talented team."

Then, as you read this vision, as you read this dream daily, life affirmations and fresh ideas will come into your mind. You will ask the question *"what can I do today toward making that happen?"* That's how you start moving.

Things are only hard if you call them hard. Label them hard, and you're right: they are hard. It's true. What you and I may think is difficult, someone else might say, that's easy. It's your perception of circumstances that really empowers them.

You may be reading this and wondering: why do I have to figure out what I love *and* get rid of what I hate to live the life that I want? It's like Seneca said, "**If one does not know to which port one is sailing, no wind is favorable.**" It's the same thing. You need to be able to believe, feel, and see the life that you are designing. You must have clearly defined goals to know where you are going. You must be able to see it in your mind. You don't need to be perfect at this; in fact, I encourage you to do it IMPERFECTLY, just start and you will get better at it. But you must *start*.

Health and fitness are a great example of where we need well-defined outcomes. For example, Grace has a goal to lose 30 pounds and get fit. She starts a fitness routine at the gym and eats healthier. But if she disconnects from these paradigm shifts, she will slide back. If you disconnect from eating well and exercising, you will slide back into unhealthy eating habits. That is a no-brainer.

It's the same thing with any change. If you don't keep your eye on what you are envisioning, then you will become disconnected from your goal. Your original paradigms are sneaky little bitches and they will come back and show their ugly heads; they will, once again, get you stuck. It is a constant lifestyle change. It gets easier over time, but we are never cured. Just like if we went on a diet and lost weight and then went back to our old eating habits. You just can't do that.

I have a friend in Whistler, B.C. who was a marketing person in that resort town, trying to get tourists to go on a sales presentation. It was fun for a while and she earned a good income, but it didn't fulfill her; she didn't love it. Now, she is living a completely different life. She dreamed up what she would love: she wanted to live in that town and make a great living. She didn't know how, but she did know what. She eventually bought a franchise. Most people would say, "I can't do that, I don't have that kind of money." That town is super-expensive by most standards, and it would be easy to run through the list of all the conditions and circumstances of why they can't. Yet, she left the marketing job and followed her dream to have her own business. At first, she got partners and investors, and then she ended up buying them out. She now lives in the town she loves, and she's got a profitable franchise. And, listen to this: She has once again sold part of the business, and hired working partners who operate her business on a daily basis. Now, her time is her own! WOOHOO!

Back in 1997–98, it looked like I had it all. I had a life that most people would have thought looked amazing. I was making a ton of money. I had a very powerful job. I was a jet-setter, which sucks, by the way, at least the way I was doing it. I was never in my home with my boyfriend or my friends or my pets—I was always in airports, hotels, or working. I was always in offices away from my home. I had big offices, big desks, and big paychecks, and, as I said earlier, I was miserable.

But one day, G.O.D. (Grand Overall Designer) gave me the insight and I unknowingly enacted the technology that I teach people now. Remember, I was at the Dallas Airport, heading back home to Seattle, and I wrote out a list. What do I want? What would I love? I didn't ask "What would I love?" back then. I didn't understand the difference between a goal and a dream. I think a goal is something you know how to get. A dream is something that you don't know how to get because it just feels so far away from you—it is just that big.

I typed a list. What do I really want? And it was only ten bullet points. When I got home, I printed it out on my dot matrix printer. (This was twenty years ago, remember!) Then I just folded up that list and put it away in a drawer. I didn't even really energize it again. If I had, I think things would have happened even faster. But what I did in making that list is bring my ideas to the surface and this gave me the clarity that I wanted. Then I put in my order with G.O.D., Spirit, Universe.

I manifested everything on my list. I got everything on my list. I decided *I will have a job where I do not have to travel all the time.* And just because that higher power has a tremendous sense of humor, I got offered a job that was 90 percent travel and a lot more money. (Of course!) But I turned that job down because it was not aligned with my vision.

I always wanted to live in Mexico. So I made a decision. I convinced my husband that we should go. I said, "Come on, let's do it! Six months, six years—let's go have an adventure." There's always a way. And we did. That was over ten years ago.

I decided that I don't want to work sixty hours a week. I want to work twenty to twenty-five hours a week. You may be thinking, "What can I do to work twenty or twenty-five hours a week and still have enough money? I don't know. But, if you did know, what could *you* do? Whatever you put your energy into, your focus makes it get bigger. That's science. That is a universal truth. What are you focusing on? Design the life you love and make a commitment to it every day.

> *Whatever you focus on, expands. If you see the world through your dreams, prosperity materializes before your very eyes. If you see the world through your fears, poverty multiplies all around you.*
>
> *Robert G. Allen*

Now, obviously, I didn't simply make the list one day and the next day my life was fine. But within one year, I went from living in Seattle to moving to Whistler, B.C., which I could have never predicted. That's where you take the "how" out of it. There's no way I could have known that I was going to break up with my terrific boyfriend of four years, meet another guy, and move to Canada.

I ended up taking a job that did not dovetail with my abilities (or my comfort, for that matter). I was invited by my new boss to Canada for a weekend of fun (I was still sad about the breakup with my boyfriend). I even tried to back out of the trip at the last minute, but she wouldn't have it. As it turned out, on that trip I met the man who became my husband ten short months later.

Get this, we went to a party. My boss introduced me to her friends, including the president of a Canadian company. Looking at me, the company president then said, "We are going to work together."

"Oh yeah. That's going to happen," I scoffed. "I'm going to quit my job and move to Canada and work for you? I don't think so. Put the crack pipe down, it's not going to happen." Yes, I really said that.

Within four months, I had moved to Whistler, was living with my new boyfriend, and working for that guy. By June 2000, my list was looking pretty good: I was now married to my Canadian boyfriend and working for the company whose president I had met earlier at that party. I got to live in a resort town and, in the slow season, I would travel. I was making great money. I was married to a man who had a great sense of humor and a tremendous sense of adventure. Everything that was on my list has happened, except for one little thing: my husband is not taller than me. I am really tall, so that is not an easy feat.

After we married and settled down, we had kids. This reminded me of my desire to live in Mexico. I wanted my children to speak Spanish. I wanted to have shorter workdays, and I didn't want the rain and gray skies that are so common in Whistler. (I was really sick of that grey drizzle part during shoulder season, which is the period between high and low season in the travel business.) Initially, my husband was very resistant, but I pointed out that I did move to Canada for him, so he kind of owed me one.

Here we are, over ten years later. We both have work that we love. We reinvented ourselves and changed our careers in our 40s. We work independently from home offices. We take our kids to school, we pick them up after. These are part of our family values. We do a lot of charity work. We are able to give in the areas where we want to give of our time, money and service.

Currently, we are making visions for the next stage of our life, and we will get it. It's an ongoing process. You don't arrive. You bring it to you, we know that writing our dreams are like living breathing documents, they will change. We are always building visions and dreams. There are always new opportunities.

If you have a vision board or a story that you write, it changes because you've manifested and created and achieved those things already. Or, you may need to redirect your story, which is okay, too. Quitting your new story and your dream is not okay. Being redirected to something that is greater for you, more in alignment with your true desire, that is cool, and it is vital to pay attention to that.

Chapter 4
COME BACK FROM THE FUTURE

There is freedom waiting for you, On the breezes of the sky, And you ask, "What if I fall?" Oh, but my darling, "What if you fly?"

Erin Hanson

What If?

What's going to happen? What if it doesn't work out? What if I am not good enough? What if I fail? What will happen if; I don't get the job, I don't get the house, I don't get the boyfriend, girlfriend, contract, health? What if I don't get the loan? What if they say no? What if I don't meet anyone? What if I can't find…

Wait…

What if it does work out? Will I have to move? Where will it be? How will I find a job, a new boyfriend, girlfriend? How will I meet people? How will I get…?

How much anxiety started to rise up when you read that piece right there? Did some of it sound familiar? Maybe this is like one of your own patterns or patterns you have seen in people you know. Over-thinking possible outcomes does not serve you.

One of the consequences of living in the future is anxiety. Often, our mind will imagine "what if" scenarios where life goes wrong. *What if I don't get the job? What if they don't like me? What if I don't have the money? The price of housing keeps going up. I'll never be able to afford it.* If you are constantly thinking too far ahead, it's going to stress you out. It will create fear and anxiety in you.

Many times, we feel the same anxiety over things *not* working out in the future as we do by them actually working out. We become worrywarts or control freaks. That's a terrible way to live: worrying, stressing, and controlling. When you find yourself in this anxious state about a possible negative future, drop the word "how."

"HOW" is a great word, but the way it is being used in this instance when you are thinking about your future life isn't serving you. Instead, it is feeding your anxiety. If you see the word "how" when you are trying to find a solution, it implies that you are at a loss and don't know what to do. In many people, when they ask "How," they are vibrating a lost and low frequency, reinforcing the feeling that there is no solution.

I am sure this is not your intention! Maybe you even want to disagree with me. That's fine, but you are the one who is currently stuck. So, what if I am right? What if what I am about to tell you will make a positive difference? Just try it on for a while. Here is what you are going to want to do: replace the "how" question with "what", trust that you are acting on a solution, and put the problem down and leave it there. (Remember, "nothing" or "I don't know" are not options for your answer.)

"What CAN I do about this situation right now?"

"What action or actions can I take in the direction of this?"

"If I could do one thing, anything right now, big or small, what action would it be?"

I carefully worded these questions. They were chosen with purpose. Let me show you what I mean.

1. "What CAN I do about this situation right now?" (Again, "nothing", is not the final answer.)

    I can … ask for help. I can bless it. I can lean into it. I can decide to not be involved. I can…

2. "What action or actions can I take in the direction of this?"

    I can put the task on my calendar to work on it head-on. I can read the book and do the research. I can visualize the desired end result, write it out, and then ask the question again. I can…

3. "If I could do one thing, anything right now, big or small, right now, in the direction of this, what would it be?" *I could make the call. I could send the message. I could design the logo. I could…*

These are all different degrees of the same question. Looking at question #3, for example, I used the word "if". It is designed to take the pressure off, which many people need to do so they can start. Just start—that is the goal of this exercise.

Here are some more examples:

How am I going to meet anyone? (You're feeling stuck.)

What could I do to meet new people? I could join an organization in the community. I could sign up for classes doing something that interests me.

How am I going to ever going to get the money? (You feel lost, confused, hopeless, and stuck.)

What is something I could do right now to generate some income?

I could sell something I own. I could ask people around me what work they need to be done. I could look for a part-time job. I could ask for more generative ideas.

Do you feel the difference in energy around asking the "what" question as opposed to the "how"?

It's okay to be imperfect. I've said it before; it is actually encouraged in this arena of life to be in motion (a.k.a.: UNstuck). You want to be *leaning in* at the very start. I am here to tell you some of the best advice I ever received was "Start imperfectly." *Start imperfectly? But what if people discover I don't know it all? What if I look foolish? What if I am found out that I am a fraud because I get stuck?* OMG, get over yourself. That is what I had to say to myself: *Sam…get real, make mistakes. Get feedback from failures and move on. Be brave and lean in. This is all in the lessons of our life's journey.*

Now, it's your turn. Grab your notebook. (Or, if you haven't downloaded the PDF go do that now at www.adesignedlifellc.com) Write out all that stuff that keeps stressing you out, those yucky little thoughts. You should dog-ear or mark this page so you can come back to it when you find yourself living in "future anxiety land" and notice those thoughts.

Don't confuse living in the future with having goals, visions, or dreams. It's not the same as designing a life that you'd love to live. You're probably thinking, "What? She was just telling me to write out a life that I'd love to live in three years, two years, or even a year from now. How I should write down what it would look like if it was all perfect. Now you are telling me not to live in the future?" Don't be confused. You need to write out what you love so that you can develop the belief and faith that this life is not only available but waiting for you. It's the map for your journey to the life you love.

Living in the future keeps you from experiencing success in the present because you are not in the now. You are missing cues. You're missing intuitions. You're missing information and opportunities. When you are not present, you're not enjoying the now. It may sound clichéd, but life is about the journey, not the destination. It is the choices that you make in the present that build the life you are envisioning.

How many times have we looked back on our life and said, "Gee, I really wish..."? That is a tool we can use by observing what we want in our life. For example, note thoughts like, "I wish I would have enjoyed that period more. I wish I would have taken advantage of opportunities or taken more pictures of my life back then. I wish I would have appreciated all that I had then." We all have points in our lives where we could look back and say, "Wow, I wasn't present for that. I didn't appreciate that as fully as I should have done."

A danger that comes from living in the future is that, sometimes, the "what ifs" we imagine can come true. We create self-fulfilling prophecies and the universe is just responding to these as it does to our requests. For example, think of a bad day. You slept through your alarm. Then you spilled coffee on your shirt and got further behind because you had to change your clothes. And just as you step on the bus, your briefcase pops open, spilling your papers and lunch all over the floor. "Oh, great!" you fume. "I knew something like this would happen. Bad things always happen in threes." Notice your words to the universe? It's responding to our thoughts. It's responding to our energy, our frequencies. Be careful what you look for because you just may find it.

In the Bible, Proverbs 23:7 states, "As a man thinks in his heart, so is he." Our thoughts are things. Everything is created twice. This is what my mentor taught me. My mentor, Mary Morrissey taught me that everything is created twice: first in thought, then in the world. Are you sitting in a chair right now? Somebody thought it up and created it before you sat down in it. It was in thought first.

The same principle is seen with the typical mental default of people who find their what-if scenarios, particularly the bad things, happening in the real world. That's the thing that keeps them stuck. They manifest it. "What if my car doesn't start?" I think the Universe and Spirit says, "Your wish is my command. Let me deliver this to you." That's called manifesting.

The thing that people should remember is that they don't manifest just the good or the bad. They manifest everything. This is not a new idea. "Stand guard at the portal of your mind," wrote Ralph Waldo Emerson in the 1800s, and it was echoed by Wallace Wattles in the early 1900s. But they are not the oldest source for this concept. Back to the Bible, Proverbs 18:21 says, "The power of life and death is in the tongue."

Why does living in the future keep us from success? It doesn't necessarily keep you from success, but when you are not in the present, you are not acknowledging or recognizing where you are and all the good that is happening at this moment. There's always good if you look for it. You can look for and believe in the good, or energize the yucky bad stuff and get more if it. It's your choice.

Where you put your attention becomes your intention. That's your signal. That's your "broadcast", as we call it. If you put your attention on gratitude, joy, on all that you *do* have, all the good in your current situation, then you are going to get more good, see more good, and feel better.

One of my best friends used to say to me when I would get on him about his perspective or attitude, "I'm a realist."

"Nope," I'd reply. "You are negative." I would tell him, "Here's the deal: you might be right. Maybe my positive point of view might be unrealistic [I didn't believe that, by the way]. But until we find out the outcome, I'm going to have a much better time on the ride."

He's going to spend that time feeling negative and dreading the future, worried and stressed, while I'm going to be running through the lily fields and singing La la la!

Symptoms You're Living in the Future

One of the most common symptoms shared by people who live in the future is worry. They are often fearful of negative consequences and anxious to maximize any positive experience. This is so prevalent in our society that we have an acronym for it: FOMO—fear of missing out.

It's true that we should avoid missing opportunities that are here today, but over-thinking about the future often means we are missing the *now*.

Staying focused on future difficulties or future fears often leads to the circumstances that make these problems happen. This tunnel vision makes people become unmotivated because they start feeling helpless or stuck.

Take, for example, my friend, Nina, who I love so much. She is a single mom. It's tough being a single mom in one of the most expensive cities in the United States. Nina wants to have her own home. She wants to buy a house, but she feels completely stuck, helpless, and even hopeless.

I'm not in her frame of mind. *I can coach her through this*, I thought. "Okay, what about this? (What would *you* suggest if you were there?) I gently probed. "Have you thought of leasing, or renting a room out to help you afford this? I wanted her to take a step in that positive direction. "What else could you do?"

But Nina totally shut down. She actually said, "I'm stuck, I feel helpless." In her mind, she made that thing in front of her bigger than what was inside of her, bigger than all that is in her corner (G.O.D., Source). She believed the lie that she was too small. HEAR ME AGAIN: There is nothing outside of you that is bigger than what you have inside of you. Whatever you are facing can never be bigger than the abilities you have within you. You have to believe that all the powers I have been speaking about so far in this book (G.O.D., Source, Universal Laws) are *inside of you*. You are not separate from them; they are part of you.

That's important for people to know. What's within them is greater than anything they face outside. If you win the battle of the mind, you can win everything else. Those fears? They're just thoughts. It's just a thought; think differently. It's just how you look at it. Your perception is how you think about it. Guess who creates your thoughts? You. Change your thinking and change your life. Is that is empowering or what?!

"Nina?" I said. "I really want you to just trust me. Look me in the eyes when I tell you this." She looked at me, nodding, her eyes were actually rimmed with tears. "There is an answer to every question. There is a solution to every problem. The thing is, your answer does not lie in the same frequency as the problem. You must get out of the problem frequency to recognize the solution frequency. If you don't, you will be STUCK in the problem. You want to be in a higher solution frequency, right?"

I put my hand on hers. "I know there's an answer to this; I know there is a solution and that's with your confidence. With your faith, I know that there's an answer. You know it too. You need to open yourself up to the possibilities of the good, of what that could be."

Just believing that, and saying out loud that there is an answer, will start bringing in ideas and possible solutions to you. It may sound insane, but if you sit there meditating on the problem, it is like you are in a pot of boiling soup. You are sitting and simmering in your problem. Get out of the pot! The answer is not inside the pot.

Changing "How" to "What's next?"

If we find ourselves lost in future worries, how do we change it? First, we must notice that we are doing it. Notice the negative thought patterns that paralyze us. Examine your thoughts and realize, hey, this isn't serving me. This isn't serving me because I am starting to notice I'm getting anxious and my mind is going down the wrong path. I often call it, "going down the rabbit hole." Start noticing if you are going down the rabbit hole.

You must begin to change your thinking. You can't just tell your brain, "Stop that." It might work for a second, but then you are going to fall back into your regular pattern because it's a habit. Remember the talk we had about "canceling that thought"? This is a reframing opportunity right here. Change your thinking. If you find yourself thinking "What if this doesn't work," then just stop your sabotage of stuckness and say, "Okay. Those thoughts aren't serving me." Instead, let's move your thinking to "What if it did work out, what would that look like? Let's energize that vision." Give your brain a task that will serve you.

What are some of the ways that it could work out? Well, we've created a dream life for ourselves already. We've created a vision. If we are worried if we are living in the future afraid of "What if they fire me? What if I don't get the job?" then one of the greatest things that you can do is to say, "Well, what if I do get the job? How would I feel if that happened? How would I act if I had the job?" Put on this new vision of your future working out as you would want. Think about how it would feel; think about how you would experience that new vision.

Again, remember there is a solution to every problem and an answer to every question. If you are looking at the future and you are getting filled with anxiety, say, "I know that there's an answer. I know that everything is happening for my better good. So, what can I do now? What is a step that I could do now to have this situation go in the direction I want it to go? What is that one thing?" (by the way, there is always a "thing you can do" big thing, teeny thing but there is always something you can do, big or small, to move in the direction of your greater good.

Lisa and Her Dream

Lisa dreamed of starting her own business. She was ready to try something new. So, as any smart person using this fluid thinking technology would do, she asked the question, "What is something I can do to move things forward?" "I know! I can design the logo and business cards!" was her first answer. That was an easy thing she could do. But then she unconsciously made things much harder than they needed to be. "If I want business cards, I am going to need to research a graphic designer," she thought.

I know Lisa pretty well, so I saw that she was making things harder than they needed to be. This was a classic example. In her mind, she has a little saboteur running in the background, as many of us do. I said, "That is definitely a thing you could do," but given her insane schedule, I continued, "When are you going to make time to research the different graphic designers? And then go sit with the different graphic designers and pour your energy into your business card? How long will it take to have the graphic designer come up with a design and get your approval? A week? Two? A month?"

Lisa was going for perfection before she could move on. Can you see how that could keep her stuck? She was waiting for the conditions to be right and setting herself up with potential delays. Trying to encourage her to keep moving forward, I said, "Great, you can totally do it that way. Let me ask you a different question. Is there another thing you could do that would move you faster and easier in the design process?" She said, "I could go online to logo design sites." Guess what? By asking another question in the moving forward program, she was able to come up with her answer, which expedited the process and got her that much closer to her goal. There is often more than one right answer, so ask again.

The Only Time is Now

There is a difference between "planning to start" and *starting*. Her plan unconsciously had her planning to start. There were a zillion obstacles that could detain making this business card. That is the little saboteur I was just talking about. As her coach, I saw this, so I had her think up a few ways to take immediate action as opposed to unconsciously sabotaging herself.

It's important to recognize that it's a question of "What can I do?", not "What should I do?" The emphasis is on your action. There is always some small step that will move you forward. Most often when you ask "Well, what should I do?", you feel a bit defeated. It's as though you are trying to qualify your action. What is a "good enough" action? Asking "What should I do?" puts a speed bump in the road to your vision because you are trying to qualify for big enough, smart enough, and perfect enough action. It slows your momentum when you are always asking "Is this good enough?"

Whatever the size of your project, it won't be as overwhelming if you break it down into smaller, manageable steps. If you look at it that way, you can even climb Mount Everest with small steps. The one objection I often hear people say is "I need to see the top of the staircase." No, you don't. Just take a step. I promise it will work—just take a step. Maybe you take three big "Mother May I" steps, and then you just take a little step. I promise at some point, if you keep going, you are going to get there, and the top step is going to reveal itself. Just know there is a top and that you will reach it. That's faith baby!

That's what I mean by the difference of asking yourself "What can I do?" because there is always something you can do. Movement in any forward direction will change your perception. Try this quick exercise: Can you see out of a window? Look straight ahead out that window right now, and notice what you can see. Okay, now move two feet to the right. When you look out the window now, has your perception changed? Do you see the view differently or something altogether new?

Yes, of course. When you feel stuck, you must change your perception. You have to move for your perception to change. The view will change when you move. You will see things differently when you move. But moving means taking action.

What I do with my clients is I ask them the questions that lead them to innovative ideas. Carol wanted to be a writer. She knew that she wanted to write books, but she didn't have thousands of dollars to spend on an online writing course. She felt stuck. "Sam, I want to write, but I have to take courses and I don't have the money. I'm so frustrated," she said.

"First, let's just assume it's all going to work out and you will be a writer," I replied. I grabbed a pen and a piece of paper. "Let's make a list of ideas. Three, maybe five ideas to help you get what you want. Okay, so what's a thing you could do? What could you do to move closer to becoming a writer?"

So, make a list. I am not asking you for the best ground-breaking idea. I am asking for an idea; for example, I could ask for help. What else could you do? I could Google ways to become a writer. Absolutely, what else could you do? I could check out a book at the library. Excellent. What else could you do? Do you see where I am going?

Carol nodded excitedly. "Just start writing every day," she said. "Exactly! You start by writing. You start by sharing. You join a writing group." That's how the process begins. You take action on your own. Keep asking what else? Are there no local writing groups? Could you start your own? Could you take part in one online? What else could you do? AND, put it in your vision "I *am* a writer", or "I have published my book."

Stop Waiting for Five Million-Dollar Ideas

That's the question. Always ask yourself, "What else could I do?" because there's always a thing. Stop waiting for the five-million-dollar idea. Instead, go for the five-dollar ideas. When you get unstuck, I can help you ask bigger questions. Because if you learn to welcome the five-dollar ideas, then you will learn to welcome the five-million-dollar ideas. The problem is that we push the five-dollar ideas away because we think that's not *the* answer. Well, here's the bottom line: the longer you wait for THE answer, the longer you are going to stay stuck. Another key word here is *waiting*. WAITING. Keep in motion, keep asking the question, and ask it differently, your answer will show up. The answer is out there (and it does exist) and when you welcome it and its friends, it will show up. (Remember, five dollar-ideas are better than no ideas.)

Ask the Question, Take the Action

People living in the future are living with circumstances and conditions, most of which are made up in their head. These circumstances might be true for someone else, but they don't have to be true for you. Having your own powerful vision and taking a step every day will lead you to a present that you always dreamed of.

For years, I had a vision of a house I wanted. But here I was in Mexico for seven years, so I didn't have the financing with U.S. or Canadian banks anymore. Financing is very different in Mexico. A mortgage in Mexico is typically only ten years, with high interest rates between 11-13 %. I could have said, "I can't do it, I don't have the money."

Instead, I stayed with the vision. I put it on my vision board. I put it in my written daily vision. "I am so happy and grateful now that I live in this beautiful house with this stunning view of the Sea of Cortez. I get to work from home."

When I asked myself, "What can I do today toward that?" G.O.D. and I collaborated, and I ended up buying the house for half of its value and at 4.5% interest on a private contract. If you believe, have a vision, and take a step every day, amazing things will start to happen. "What could I do?" turned into "I am going to contact an owner and ask if they are interested in carrying the note." That's an action.

"I can't change careers because I won't make enough money." "Even if I did, I would have to commute, and how will I take care of my kids?" These thoughts are designed to keep you stuck. Ask yourself an action question. "What can I do that I love and make money?" Get out of the problem.

Always take action. Don't worry about it; just know it's going to happen and ask, "What can I do today? What can I do now?" There's always something. A lot of times you must rely on God, Spirit, Universe, or Source to reveal it to you. But They can't reveal it to you until you get further down the path.

Chapter 5
THE PAST IS THE PAST, LET'S LEAVE IT THERE

> *If you are depressed, you are living in the past.*
> *If you are anxious, you are living in the future.*
> *If you are at peace, you are living in the present.*
> **Lao Tzu**

Why is living in the past so appealing to people? There are many reasons. Sometimes, it's appealing because we recall our life in the past as being great; life seemed simpler and easier—we were more carefree. We tend to over-glamorize the way things were.

Or, if life was difficult, some people may enjoy getting attention for a sad or difficult story. Their suffering gets them attention. People respond to them with kindness and sympathy: "Oh, that's terrible," and "Oh, my goodness, you poor thing." Attention feels good, so they focus on what gets them attention. It's not a conscious choice. They don't wake up in the morning, saying, "Hey, I think I'm going to go and tell my story to people to have them give me attention." But it is an effective way to get attention. And the "hit" of sympathy from each retelling can be addictive.

Neural Linguistic Programming (NLP) will tell you that there is an emotional anchor to this, meaning that certain experiences from your past have strong emotions tied with them. An example of this would be the loving feelings that are triggered when you smell cookies baking and you think, "Christmas at Grandma's house." A negative version of this could be refusing to wear your green shirt because you were wearing it on the day that you had the breakup fight with your ex. I think one cure for these negative anchors is to acknowledge that it *has* happened, then just say, "Not this time," and step out into the present and re-anchor with something lovely and present.

The Value of the Past: Reflection

Having said all that, there are benefits from reflecting on our past. If we decide to look at it as a learning opportunity, there are great lessons to be learned. If we can analyze the past without emotion clouding our judgment, we can ask valuable questions: What would I do differently? How could I do better in the future? We can analyze something in the past and say, "I loved that! I'd like to create more of this in my life right now. What can I do today to bring that experience into the now?"

We can look at the past as a gift, regardless. It is an opportunity to show gratitude. Many people use the phrase, "I'm so grateful for…" and list aspects of their life that they appreciate. "I'm so grateful for my comfy bed. I'm so grateful for my car, my health. I'm so grateful for a roof over my head. I'm grateful for my family."

We have the other type of reason to be grateful: for a less desirable or even negative experience. When you reflect on your past, acknowledge and recognize that you were hurt at the time, but it has given you some new and valuable information and experiences to move forward.

For example, you might say, "You know what? That job interview sucked, but I am so glad I learned my lesson. What I am taking from that experience is that I am going to go to my next interview having researched the company thoroughly." That is how to gain the lesson from the past: reflect on what happened (good or bad) and think, "What can I take from that experience? What can I do better the next time?"

I often tell my clients that when they are in regret or remorse about something in their past, they can get a little stuck there. I say, "Let me ask you this question: faced with the same situation today, would you make the same decision again?" If the answer is no, then it's time to let it go. No. Perfect, let it go, the lesson is learned. Be thankful for the learning, be thankful for the gift, and move on.

What can the past teach you? It teaches you what you *do* want and what you *don't* want. If we are in the business of designing our lives, rather than living by default, then we take all of these experiences and we glean the lessons from them and move forward. If you do not, then you are just passively letting life "happen" to you, rather than actively living a life you love.

The Problems with Living in the Past

Depression is one of the biggest problems associated with living in the past. Often, people remember the past as being problem-free. They over-glamorize what it was. When they are confronted with new challenges in the present, feelings of being overwhelmed can lead to them to retreat to the comforting memories of the past.

Looking back on what was and what could have been is a recipe for depression. *Why did I make that decision? Why did I move there? Why did he do that to me? I remember when we used to have fun. I wonder what the ex is up to now?* (If you are married or in a relationship, that last one is a huge opportunity for disaster, by the way.) Can you change the past? Nope! So, what can you do with it? That depends on whether the memory is helpful in some way (serving you), or if it is hurting you. If it is a serving memory, like sitting and eating berries with Grandma or remembering a past success that reminds you that you are a capable person, then, yes! These are GOOD memories. These good and happy memories are a source of strength.

But successful, serving memories are not what I am referring to here. I am talking about the crappy energies of regret or shame. To feel regret or shame is important for your personal growth, *in the moment*. If I am to be totally honest, most of my best lessons in life were learned the hard way. I made a bad decision or choice. It hurt, and since I don't like to hurt, now I don't repeat it. That's the trick: to feel it ONCE, to learn from it, and move on. To repeat it or run the scenario over and over in your head is abuse. Every time you run that program, you are essentially saying, "I am stuck, and I don't deserve better." Is it any wonder why you feel depressed?

Look for the Lesson

The good news is that there's a way out of repeating those painful, negative memories. Look for the lesson in every experience. Ask yourself:

what is the good in the situation? There is ALWAYS a silver lining. Always. What did you learn? The learning is the gift!

Another difficulty people face when they live in the past is that they get stuck. They don't make changes or decisions because they are tied to the illusion of keeping everything as it used to be. They find comfort through the familiar, even if it will eventually harm them. They don't show up to day-to-day life because they are holding onto an image of what was.

It's like the Garth Brooks' song that he sings about his high school sweetheart called "Unanswered Prayers." It's about how this girl was his "be-all and end-all." He thought that he couldn't go on without her, his high school sweetheart, yadda, yadda, yadda, and then, years later, he runs into her when he is out with his wife. Then he realizes that he is grateful for the unanswered prayer, that the girl he thought he loved in high school wasn't it.

Wishful thinking statements are often signs that people prefer living in the past rather than dealing with issues. "If I only knew," becomes their mantra, an explanation for their circumstances. Now we are talking about paradigms (and we all know, paradigms can be sneaky little bitches.)

Sometimes, depression will cause us to focus on the negative energy of loss. "I don't have that. I'm living there, so I don't have that." Or it turns into a pity party—"Poor little me." Or it turns into a story of "You don't know what happened to me." When we say those comments, when we put those phrases out there, energetically speaking, they feel really yucky. They feel really low. "Boy, if you knew what happened to me, this is why I am this way. This is why I can't…" Remember, we get more of whatever frequency we are vibrating at, so making these negative, low-energy statements pulls us downward, thus increasing the depressed, low-energy feelings. Do you want to see where your thoughts are? Take a look at your life because your thoughts, good or bad, are manifesting and creating all the time.

> *Your mind is a garden. Your thoughts are the seeds.*
> *You can grow flowers, or you can grow weeds.*
> ***Author Unknown***

We know that when we think too much about the future, it is anxiety-driven. "What's going to happen to me?" we ask. If we look closer at that, let's examine another question: what's the opposite of "What's going to happen"? Living-in-the-past thinking is driven by sadness and depression. You use phrases like "You don't know what happened. I have experienced so much loss. I have experienced so much greatness; I don't know if I can repeat it." These are just low-frequency thoughts.

If you get into habitual self-undermining phrases like "I'm not good at this because history has shown so far, I am not good with money… I'm not good with men. I am not good with technology. I am not good with…" These phrases become self-limiting beliefs that trap you into depression and keep you stuck. But the truth of the matter is that at any given time, once you decide to act, you can change your perspective.

People say similar things to me all the time: "I'm not good with money", "I'm not good with technology", and "I'm not very good with people." I tell them, "Okay, let's stop that, right there. Let's go ahead and draw a line in the sand and say, 'I used to be bad with money, but now I am…'" And then we rephrase the thought right then and there to transform it into a positive, energizing thought. "I used to be bad with money, but now I am getting better at it every day." The first change is to make the negative statement a comment on past events: "I *wasn't* good with people", "I *used* to have problems with men." Next, add the modifying phrase, "But now," and then tell your new story. "I used to be terrified at the thought of speaking in public, *but now* I can give a presentation to a room full of people without any problem."

I tell people that I used to be addicted to dating alcoholics. Alcohol wasn't my problem; I just loved all the symptoms of alcoholics (this could be another book altogether on all the characteristics of alcoholism or its symptoms. It ain't just the booze, kids.) I was an active, super co-dependent, and I was drawn to take care of them; it made me feel needed and important. But not anymore. No sirree! I used to…and in my case, it is currently my actual truth.

Past Memories Hurt Present Relationships

How does living in the past affect the relationships you have with others? Living in the past is a habit that can set you up for disappointment. How is this affecting your relationships? Do the people, places, and things have a chance at stacking up to your memories? Has your past been so glamorized that your present can't compete? Or has the present been so drained of positive energy that you can't get out of bed? Are you weighed down with thoughts like, "My old boyfriend did *this*. My old job was like that. My boss was like this. My old apartment was like this. My house was like this."? How does anybody have a chance to compete? It's like Theodore Roosevelt said, "Comparison is the thief of joy."

Larry's Story

When you have these experiences of lessons or gifts of the past, they become stepping stones, not only for yourself to move forward but also for others. I have discovered this lesson to be a biggie!

Let me tell you about Larry. Larry had a thriving business. He loved his customers, they adored him, and he was truly engaged in his work. Larry made plenty of money and was very successful. He was well-regarded in his community.

Some time ago, Larry cheated on his wife of twenty years. They had three children and what most would consider a happy marriage. Yet, he made a mistake. He knew it was wrong, he knew it was a mistake, but he went against his better judgment and did it anyway. His wife found out. His mistress got pregnant and he ended up fathering a child. That's it, marriage over.

The relationship with his mistress didn't work out, and they are no longer together. Now he is estranged from his older children and raising a toddler.

Larry had so much guilt, remorse, and shame. He lost his marriage, he lost respect and trust in the community, he lost a lot of business, and he was *stuck*. He was depressed and looking for ways of punishing himself. He played out a small life for a long time. He moved into a trailer, moved from job to job, and eventually started a business. But rather than making it the best (which he knew how to do), he got distracted into other business ideas and other jobs. He was disinterested in having all that he was capable of having because he was living in the past of *what was*. Larry was actually unconsciously punishing himself. Somehow, Larry thought that by creating a miserable life for himself (because guilt made him feel undeserving of happiness), he would make things better with his kids and ex-wife.

You gotta know, that is not how it works. Pushing the good away from you because you don't feel deserving is not serving anyone. It doesn't serve you, your family, your boss, or your friends.

I am happy to say, years later, that Larry is figuring it out.

NOW, he is best friends with his ex-wife, who is happily remarried. NOW, he makes time to recognize, spend quality time, and adore *all* his kids. Now, he participates regularly with activities supporting his church. Now, he is writing a book to help others navigate life after infidelity.

Did Larry have a reason to feel shame? Absolutely! Was choosing to play it small and punishing himself for eight years serving him? No, not really. it robbed a lot of people of his gift of himself, of his potential, of his giving, loving, successful self. The silver lining? Larry is back and better than ever, living a life worthy of him and helping others.

How do people stop living in the past? The best, healthiest way to stop living in the past is to look at it for what it is. You bless your past. Honest to goodness, the good, the bad, and the ugly. You are grateful for it. And then you let it go.

First, you develop an awareness of when you are living in the past. You must acknowledge when a thought is no longer about your present situation but is a circumstance from the past. Ask yourself the question: What is this? What is this thought trying to teach me, so I can move on? You need to ask deep questions if you want to break and re-pattern paradigms. As we progress through this book, remember that "I don't know" is not a sufficient answer. You don't get to say, "I don't know."

Suffering is (kinda) Selfish

Many times, when you are stuck in the past, there is a bit of suffering around it, including loss-- suffering from not having something. It's really kind of self-centered. Now, I am talking about habitual suffering, not short-term hurts or pains. I am talking about the holding on and on and on. There's nothing outward we are giving when we are energizing our suffering. When you are suffering, when you are sitting in this trap, you can't be available for others. You're always trying to get onto the subject of what's going on with you and how things aren't working *for you*. You always direct the conversation, whether in your head or with others, back to your problems. You are perpetuating Stuckness. I guarantee you that this isn't going to lead to a better life.

It's heartbreaking for me to see people truly stuck. Because it is paralyzing, and the past we talk about creates this low vibration within us, it can lead to depression. What's possible in the real world will never (in their mind) measure up to their glamorized memory of what once was. However, I think there's always a reason. Feelings of guilt for causing someone emotional pain, guilt for staying in a bad or abusive relationship, or even guilt for moving on if a loved one passed away.

Denise is another example of someone who became paralyzed by the past. Denise loved her husband, James, like crazy, but he was a really difficult man. His habitual drinking and gambling addiction made many of their years together hard. Denise was 20 years younger than James, and when James passed away, she wanted to go have her life; she wanted to travel and socialize. But her mind was not honoring her present situation. It was stuck in the past and paralyzing her with thoughts like, "I don't know how to do this." She became depressed because she didn't know how to reinvent herself. You may know people in this situation—it could even be you. It takes support, it takes blessing the past, honoring it, and then putting it where it belongs. It takes a vision and constant belief that a life you can love again is available to you, and then it takes action.

Remember, movement changes your perception. Whether you move physically, mentally, or emotionally, when you move, you open yourself to changing your perception. Just like the window exercise in Chapter 3, imperfect steps are moving us to new learning experiences, helping us get out of our drama, and allowing us to reinvent ourselves. People do it all day long. I did it. You've done it. We all do it. Guess what? Anyone can reinvent themselves when they are not stuck.

Exercise: *Step into the Present*

What are some ideas or beliefs from your past that might be keeping you stuck? These can be beliefs that, logically, you know shouldn't matter now, but emotionally and energy-wise, these things are playing a role in keeping you stuck.

Let's reframe them and put them where they belong. It's time to get your PDF notebook out (www.adesignedlifellc.com) and open it to a fresh page. On the left, write the old stuff. On the right, let's reframe them to tell your new story, your truth.

Old Stuff	Reframe

Start Where You Are

You have an opportunity to be filled with hope when you are living in the present. You can be emotionally available for those you love and others around you. You can make a difference. Getting yourself happy in your own life – living a life that you love isn't just for you, trust me. It's for everyone in your life. You will become more available to people. You will live a richer, brighter life. People who you don't even think are paying attention will look at you and say, "Wow, what a difference" like the restaurant scene in the movie *When Harry Met Sally*: "I want some of what she is having!"

Be present, sleep better, and know it's all working out. These are all behaviors of someone who is present and in gratitude. See, when you live in the present, you can be grateful for where you are right now, period.

I think living in the past is like holding a piece of coal, and I was the one that was getting burnt. That is the danger—you may think that it's keeping you warm, but you are holding on to something that is just burning you. It's not serving you. Love it and release it. The good, the bad, and the ugly—love it, bless it, and release it. Thank you for the lessons.

Chapter 6
THE ONLY TIME IS NOW

*Happiness is not something you postpone for the future;
it is something you design for the present.*
Jim Rohn

Will you ever have the perfect conditions to change your life? You're thinking, "Probably not." I know NOW is always the perfect time, but change can be difficult. Many people will say that they hate change, or that change is too hard. It sounds like the truth for us because our paradigms are so strong. Our narratives, our old familiar stories, are strong because we have told them so often that we believe they must be true.

If we address the conditions needed to create change, we will see a change in our lives. We will create the circumstances where change is possible: "I will move when *x happens*", "I will get the new job when *y happens*", "I will start saving money for retirement when…" The truth is that you need to start doing it first, then the conditions will change. People often have the misconception that it's the conditions that make things possible when really, YOU make things possible by changing the conditions.

The law of attraction has the word "action" right in it! You go first. You must go first. It's responding to you. If you are waiting to respond to it, it's merely mirroring who you are today, right now. That's how it works. So, if you are in an old, stuck state, the law of attraction says, "Okay, I will stay stuck with you. Oh! You are moving? Great! You are doing something different. Well, let me get on that; let me match your vibration!" That's how the law of attraction works.

Think about consistency and momentum. Consistency and momentum are BFFs. Momentum is a big shot. He is the guy that is going to propel you forward, and he is going to propel you forward fast. But you will never get to meet Momentum unless you become best friends with Consistency first.

Consistent action is movement in the direction of your vision or dreams. Consistent action is taking little steps, big steps, tiny steps, and giant "Mother may I" steps to get you down the path, closer and closer to living the life you love. The conditions will probably never be perfect. And if they are, you might miss the moment and get complacent. When the conditions are perfect, we get comfortable again.

I worked with a few clients recently that had to face some very hard lessons. Old programs were running, and they suffered through learning the hard way. It's easy for me to sit here in my comfy seat on the other side of my own tough times and say, yep, I didn't learn my lessons easily either. The way you feel right now really is no fun. Lesson learned. You can stay the victim in it or you can say, "Ouch! I don't want to feel that way again. So, I am going to be different; I am going to respond differently." Don't react, respond.

It can be tempting to think that you can never get out of your bad situation. You feel deep doom and gloom. One of my clients is a coach and she took an absolute pity party nose-dive. (Surprise, coaches have life issues, too.) We all run into our own paradigms. We all run into our past, and there are times when therapy is needed. Sometimes the issues are deep.

My goal as a coach is to ask probing questions so people will come up with deeper answers than they have done in the past. At some point in their lives, they had gotten used to a simple explanation, something such as, "I can't change now. It's just who I am." But if you ask the right questions, their entire vision starts to reset. Often, it happens in an instant. They hear themselves saying, "Oh, I think I just figured it out!" That's my role as a coach. My role isn't to find out why you are afraid of water or to remind you the reason you are afraid of water is that you almost drowned when you were two and, thus, energize the problem. My role is to tell you that your answer exists. It is already inside you, so let's find it together and move toward it. Let's get back in the water now; you are no longer two years old. Let's swim!

The Lean-In Approach

On my desk, I keep a little flashlight. I wish I had this little flashlight when I was younger. At times, we may think we are awake in the middle of the night and think we see a boogeyman in the closet, and we are paralyzed with fear. *What is that? Is it going to get me?* Eventually, we wake up and our rational mind tells us nothing is there. But if we had a flashlight on the nightstand and quickly shone it into the closet, we would have seen right away that there's nothing there to fear.

Now I use that flashlight to shine in the closet; I shine it in every corner, proving that there's nothing there. Test your fear. Lean into it. You are going to find out that you are most likely making it much bigger than it really is. There is nothing outside of you that is bigger than the power that is within you.

You were created personally by an Incredible Power. God's Great Universe has made you with amazing personal power. You just have to have faith in your ability to overcome the fear that is gripping you. That's the lean-in approach. Take action. How do I get started? Do anything. Take any action toward your vision, leaning into the fear and lighting up the corners.

Pick up the phone. Make the call. That's the best.

I am kind of a hard ass in this department. For example, I have a client, Paige, who works in sales. Paige has a list of clients she needs to contact to grow her business, but she is afraid that her clients will think that her new products are too expensive, and she is worried that she will lose their business. Paige is anxious about the future. "What if my clients respond this way?" she thinks. So, she keeps putting off calling them.

I have often seen this happen with clients in the past. One successful solution that I have used before with clients takes place while we are Skyping or on Facetime in our session. I tell them to pick up the phone and call their clients immediately (as in, right <u>now</u>!) I will actually ask them to do it in that moment. I don't let them off the hook. SHINE THE LIGHT. If we don't do it right then and there, we'll put it off for later. If there's something unenjoyable about a task, we will procrastinate and avoid it. Many times, your resistance toward doing something right now is simply inertia. Fear inflates the task and turns it into the boogeyman in your closet. Doing the task right away is like shining the flashlight into the dark closet. The boogeyman isn't there, and if there is an obstacle—big deal! Move through it. I promise that you are going to be fine, whatever it is.

Maybe you will call and find out you didn't get the job. Okay, it wasn't for you. What were the things about that job that you loved? What about it did you dislike? Were you settling? Perhaps it feels as if it was ideal. Great! Then you tell the Universe, "That was my ideal job and I want something just like that." Now you start searching, knowing that you are partnered with God/Spirit/Universe.

> *Great things are done by a series of small things brought together.*
> **Vincent Van Gogh**

Romans 8:28 states: "*And we know that all things work together for good to those who love God, to those who are the called according to His purpose.*" The part that always gets me is that "all things work together for good." So, when you don't get that job, there's something better waiting. It is all for the greater good. Many people have a hard time believing that. They stay in fear mode. To lean into something means to step toward faith. When I say faith, I'm speaking about having faith that everything is going to work out. Faith is the greatest part of the lean-in. Lean in and shine that light.

If I told you that you have a choice between faith or fear, which one would you consciously choose right now? Of course, we all would choose faith. Faith is leading the energy that it is all going to work out. Fear is blocking and driving the energy down. Remember that Faith and Fear do not coexist, meaning you can't have both at the same time. So, pick one!

Going back to our example of the phone call, let's say that you are my client and you chose to have faith that everything would work out as planned. What would you be doing right now? You would make the call.

Again, let's just say it did work out. You took a step, acting in faith, and you were rewarded. What do you do after that? What's your next best move? Notice my wording here: it wasn't what's my next move, it's what's my next *best* move? Just figure out the next best move, not the overall perfect move.

Remember, we talked earlier about striving for perfection and getting so hung up on the details with the result that we don't do anything. Go ahead, do it imperfectly. What's one of your next best moves? It doesn't have to be one answer. It could be seventy-three little answers.

Lean In: Crisis Time

What if you are dealing with a crisis now, and all you can do is react? How can the lean-in approach help?

One of the greatest tools we can use in this instance is to stop and decide how we respond to the crisis. We have a choice: we can either react or respond. When you react, you don't think. I picture reacting like when you get a bug bite and your skin swells up. Or if someone threw a stick at you, you try to bat it away. Those are reactions, not responses. The problem with a reaction is that you cannot be sure that what you are deciding is going to be a good choice.

A response has much calmer energy. Responding is faith energy, rather than fear energy. If you know that you are the designer of your life and your life is going to work out, then the Universe, God, and Spirit will purely respond to you, your requests, and your frequency. I love this tool. Do you hear what I am telling you? I am telling you that all of that is responding to you. You must get into response mode, not reaction mode.

So, back to being in crisis mode. Eventually, everyone has these moments—how do I respond, rather than react? I stop. I look at the crisis from a distance: if I knew it was all going to work out and I looked back at this moment six months from now, what would my future self tell me in the crisis moment? Chill out, it's fine. That was a crazy time, but it all worked out.

Take the Charge Out of the Situation

It's your turn to make breakfast for the kids and now the smoke detector is going off because the toaster was set to extra dark. The alarm is wailing, and your five-year-old son starts crying because the noise frightens him. Do you shout at him, telling him that he should handle it maturely? Do you run around the kitchen, screeching? No, course not. Those are actions that would increase the stress and add to the problem. You want to take the charge *out* of the crisis. You take the batteries out of the smoke detector and open the window to clear the air. (Of course, you put the batteries back once the smoke has cleared. Safety first!) Remove the power from the things that are in your control to reduce your stress. In that moment, the smoke detector was not serving you, so you took the power away from the thing that was creating the crisis.

If you step out of your story for a moment and look around, you will find that you almost always know how to handle crisis moments. You have that intuition. It's been sourced to you through G.O.D. all along. You just didn't listen. If you say, "I am taking the batteries out", there is no longer a charge to that situation. You can move through it with faith. I am going to act in faith. You don't curl in a ball, go fetal, and suck your thumb. That doesn't work. Take a step forward and shine the light.

Think of your thoughts as conduits, like hoses interconnecting in your mind. In crisis mode, you have a kink in the "I can handle things" hose and the tap is turned full on with the "I only run on chaos" hose. You have to turn off the flow to the "chaos" hose and unkink the "I can handle things with ease hose" to increase your sense of deserving and your ability to respond to the crisis. Because in most instances, the problems that we label "crises" are simply a matter of perception.

Part of the message that keeps coming to me about this is what if it did work out? Let's just energize that. Let's just say it's working out. Now what? This is an awesome tool.

Lean into the Fear

Fear is not only an emotion but a powerful feeling throughout your body. Your mouth goes dry and your palms sweat. You may feel weak, have butterflies in your stomach, or other symptoms as your body goes into fight or flight mode. With all of these reactions happening that seem out of your control, it can make fear seem incredibly hard to resist.

But as overwhelming as these symptoms can be, fear is merely feedback. Start thinking of it that way and life will get a whole lot easier and faster. The anxiety that you feel when you are afraid to call the guy is feedback. The heart-pounding moments before your big presentation is feedback. Fear is just telling you to shine a light on whatever is triggering those reactions. Let's see what they really are. Fear is not proof that you can't do something; it's feedback that you haven't done it *yet*. Maybe you haven't done it successfully, but it's not evidence that you can't do it.

> *Whether you think you can, or you think you can't—you're right.*
> **Henry Ford**

The truth in fear is that you have the choice. It's a double-sided coin: on one side of the coin is fear and on the other side is faith. I don't want to live in fear. Living in constant fear sucks. Fear hurts, and it stops growth. Fear plays a large part in staying stuck.

Let me be clear: there are two types of fears, and I am talking about the paralyzing kind that keeps us stuck. I'm not talking about useful fear like, "The stove's hot. I am afraid I am going to get burned." Okay, then back away from the stove, don't touch the burner. That's common-sense fear that keeps you safe. We need to shine a light on our paralyzing fear, step toward it, and expose it for what it is: a lie that keeps us from living a life we love. Decide to use faith instead of fear. Open yourself to the possibilities that arise when we say, "What if it works?"

Start from where you are with what you have and do it right now. Don't wait for conditions to improve so things can get better for you; make them better by improving yourself. Let me explain: you need to LEAN IN when you feel like shutting down, procrastinating, or backing off. When fear and doubt show up, step forward and *lean into it*. This is where the magic happens. The life you really want resides outside your comfort zone. It's true! There is a big, fat, juicy life waiting for you, but you have to move into it. You must ask the question you learned earlier. *What CAN I do, from where I am, with what I have, right now?* Even the smallest baby steps will start you on a path out of awful, sucky stuckness. There is *always* something you can do, ALWAYS. (Remember the cookie recipe? Don't omit an ingredient here!)

Currently, you are most likely living in a world of circumstances and conditions. This, my friend, is partly the reason why you are stuck. So how about trusting me, or better yet, trust G.O.D. How about trusting the laws of the universe? Let's do it this way for a while; I know this works. If you have doubts, let's put them aside for now and you can borrow MY knowing. Face it, you really have nothing to lose and everything to gain.

First, I am going to unwrap exactly what I mean by circumstances and conditions. You are basing your life decisions on what you are currently experiencing, or on what is going on around you. By doing this, you let your beliefs about things be dictated to you.

Let me give you some examples. Anyone reading this book has lived through a drop or dip in the economy. During these periods, people freak out about how broke everyone is and they say things like, "The economy is broken and we can't buy a house; we can't change jobs or make a move; we may lose all our money; other people lost their money, so that must mean the same for us." This is a recipe to stay stuck and paralyzed!

Did you know that the worst economic times have been when the most millionaires are made? It must be because they are so smart, rich, and educated, right? Well, maybe. It's more likely they didn't allow other people's stories or the doom and gloom of their perceptions to rule them. These entrepreneurs became millionaires because they leaned into WHAT they could do and took action.

Here is a cool insight from David Yetman's blog on this particular issue:

Not everyone suffered during the Great Depression. More people became millionaires during this time than in any other time in American history. Opportunities, that were not present during the 1920s economic boom times, suddenly became available. An economic downturn is a good time to start a business. Start-up costs are much lower in a recession than in boom periods. Savvy entrepreneurs edged in and positioned themselves for when the economic climate improved.

In Kentucky, a grandfather called Colonel Sanders started serving fried chicken at his gas station. By 1937, he had expanded to a 142-seat restaurant due to popular demand. Two young electrical engineering graduates stared an electrical machine business in a rented garage during the 1930s. Bill Hewlett and Dave Packard officially became business partners in 1939 with only $538 in investment money. (Yetman 2016)

The following is a story from *A Gift of Inspiration*, and it has always stayed with me. It is the perfect example of giving power to and giving into conditions and circumstances. Your perception is your truth.

The Man Who Sold Very Good Hot Dogs

There was once a man who lived by the side of the road and sold hot dogs. He was hard of hearing, so he had no radio - he had trouble with his eyes, so he read no newspapers and of course he didn't look at television. But he sold very good hot dogs. He put up signs on the highway telling everyone how good they were, he stood on the side of the road and cried out to all that past "Buy a hot dog, they are the best in town."

And people bought his hot dogs and he increased his meat and bun orders. He bought a bigger stove to take care of all the extra business. He finally got his son to come and help him out with his business.

But then something happened, his son who had been well educated said… "Father, haven't you been listening to the radio or reading the newspapers or watching television? There's a big recession happening right now. The current business situation is terrible in this country - we have problems with unemployment, high living costs, strikes, pollution, the influence of minorities and majorities, the rich, the poor, drugs, alcohol, capitalism and communism."

Whereupon his father thought, "Well, my son's been well educated. He reads the papers, listens to the radio and watches television, so he ought to know."

So his father cut down on his meat and bun orders, took down all his advertising signs and no longer bothered to stand by the side of the road to promote and sell his hot dogs… and his hot dog sales fell almost overnight.

"You're right, son," the father said. "We certainly are in the middle of a recession." Author Unknown (Ready 2015)

I would like to add a note to this. I am not suggesting you deny the facts of what is happening around you. I am, however, telling you to deny the power you give those facts in your life. I am suggesting you write your own truths, your own stories around how you want to feel, live, and be in any given situation.

Believe it, decide on it, and step into it. If you can't believe it in its entirety right now, can you believe in part of it? Start to believe even in its slight possibility. You don't need absolute belief to start the process of conscious manifesting. You can start by really getting behind that which you do believe is possible and energize the heck out of that part! After you read the examples of people who stayed in their belief, you will want to write down *your* learning point or takeaway from the story after each one. I will give you a simple example after the story of J.K. Rowling.

J.K. Rowling

Before she became a multi-millionaire bestselling author, J.K. Rowling experienced deep pain in her personal life: the death of her mother, a failed marriage and depression. It may sound unlikely, but it was at that time when she felt most hopeless that she began to write the story of a boy who was also trapped in desperate circumstances --and his magical escape--Harry Potter.

After her manuscript was rejected multiple times, no one would have blamed Rowling for giving up. But she knew that she had to share her creation with the world. Her determination and self-belief eventually led to Harry Potter becoming an international best-seller, an eight-movie franchise (and counting) a theme park and more! It seems like there are a lot of people hoping for a little more magic in their lives.

Takeaway/learning points: She is an inspiration; if she can do it, so can I. She gave the gifts of escape, imagination, and fantasy to people through her books. Adults and children could bond and have family enjoying her series. She was a huge giver. So many would not have benefited from her philanthropy, had she stayed stuck.

Procrastination Paralyzes

What does procrastination look like in your life? For me, it usually started by procrastinating on dealing with my tendency to procrastinate! I would plan to make plans. I think of things that I should be doing, but I'm not. Then I beat myself up for a while because I should have been doing it. That soaks up more of my time! Can anyone else relate???

When you procrastinate on a task, as I said before, it's usually because it's something that you find undesirable. (Duh! That's for sure.) We don't want to do things that we don't like. But, "undesirable" also has subcategories because maybe there is some fear tied to the task. What if it doesn't work out? It leads right back into those feelings of being afraid. The reason doesn't have to be logical or deep; it could be something plain and simple. What if I don't like it? But by *leaning in,* by saying, "I'm in, put me in the game, coach," you push past procrastination paralysis.

Leaning in lets you push past the resistance of procrastination and you learn that it was never as big as you thought it was, and now it's behind you. For example, the sooner you get into the rhythm of a job, the sooner you get through it, and the sooner you get done. Once it's behind you, you will feel a sense of pride. We often forget that there is a reward on the other side of a task. There's a pick-up in self-esteem that comes from completion.

The residual effect that comes from beating procrastination can be very positive. By just tackling the task, you are taking back your power and sense of control. I have a highly effective tool that I use to beat my own tendency to procrastinate. It's called "calendarizing." Yes, it is a made-up word and idea that someone taught me, and I now preach it to all my clients!

The only cure for procrastination is for you to fall in love with your calendar. And, I have to tell you, it was a BIG transition for me to go digital! It was a major transition to trust my laptop and my phone to sync. I started calendarizing on my computer, and then I would print my weekly calendar so I had the paper version (old habits sometimes die hard). But after two years of printing, I have been 100% digital and synching for a long time now. There is hope for you too.

There are many successful ways of calendarizing. Here is one of my favorites: you say, it's not reasonable for me to organize and tidy my office right now, it's a giant project. I am going to grab my pen and write on April 3 and April 6 from 1:00 to 3:00 p.m. I am going to be in the office cleaning and organizing. Here's the important part: you put it in your calendar and then you also make that appointment with your friend who is going to come and help de-clutter. Make the task a commitment to a friend and the job gets done. If you can't rope a friend in, keep the commitment to yourself, just like you would if your friend were able to come and they chose to take their precious time to show up and help you. If they did show up to help you, then you wouldn't lay on the couch watching TV and say, "Yeah, sorry, I don't feel like it, but thanks for coming anyway." (SUPER RUDE)

As for calendarizing, it may sound crazy, but I suggest you do this with everything. I went back in my files and I looked at an old calendar where I even scheduled quiet time with my kids seven years ago. Their nap time became my down-time to be a mom with my kids in the middle of my day. Fall in love with the calendar. Come Sunday night, open up that calendar, look at your week, and check your plans. What needs to be moved? What needs your attention? What needs confirmation? Live by it and color-code it to make it work for you.

Let your calendar help you make decisions: do not accept an engagement or additional work without checking the calendar. People who tend to procrastinate will wait until the night before they see me to check the tasks in their calendars because they know I am going to kick their asses if they don't do what they said. *Oh, this needs to be done tomorrow. I need to do it.* Accountability is a good repellant for procrastination.

Let's use the example of Juan procrastinating cleaning his office. What is an action that he could take? His office was a disaster. It had so much stuff everywhere that he barely had a place to sit! He was avoiding his office because it didn't feel good. It bummed him out to be in it.

Juan had a giant pile of paperwork on his desk that he kept promising to deal with "later." After one coaching session, Juan realized he was tired of walking past that damn pile of paper. He finally buckled down and got through it. His office now looks amazing! Every time he walks into his office, he feels so good, lighter, like he had been holding his breath before every time he walked past that mountain of paperwork.

Often when we are procrastinating, excuses get in our way. Claiming to be disorganized is another reason to procrastinate. People like to use phrases like "I'm just so busy" to explain why they haven't done anything. That's a typical reason why people procrastinate. We can call it an excuse or a reason, but "I'm just so busy" is often just procrastination dressed in business clothes. But if you really wanted to do something, if it sounded appealing to you, you would be ready to go and make space for it in a heartbeat!

Can you tell? I am a giant fan of calendarizing. I think it's a fantastic habit to get into every day. Feeling overwhelmed comes from trying to handle too many tasks, like a circus juggler spinning plates and they are starting to fall. So, when someone says they are too busy to organize, they are missing the truth: if they got organized, they wouldn't be so busy.

We all have the same number of hours in a day, and we need to organize our tasks to fit them. People tend to be very optimistic about how quickly they can get things done. You think, "Okay, I put this on my calendar, but it took way longer." Then you know next time you put it on your calendar, that job takes much longer than you first thought. Remember, it's a learning process and a skill that you must polish over time. Stop being a victim of "I'm just so busy" thinking. Organize your calendar. Get the thoughts and to-do's off your brain and shoulders and put them in their place at the appropriate time on your calendar. Fall in love with it and create space to live the life you love.

Circumstances and conditions affect the NOW but don't make them bigger than you. When you make them bigger than you, you'll get stuck. When you make what's going on outside of you bigger than what's inside, you are giving away your power, which creates procrastination, fear, and crisis. Remember to shine a light on it. Use your calendar as a powerful tool to tame your own circumstances and conditions. Circumstances and conditions are not going to change for you until you change first. It's time for action!

Chapter 7
DO YOU REALLY KNOW?

If you don't stand for something, you will fall for anything.
Gordon A. Eadie

Many people can see the obstacle(s) that keep them stuck, but they get lost in the fog of phrases like "Yeah, I know that," and live powerless lives. I have coached people who know what their next step should be, but when I prompt them to take that step, they say, "Oh, I know that. I should do better, and I know that." This kind of rationalizing looks good on the surface, but if you dig a little deeper, it's the same BS that has you staying stuck. It's dangerous because it keeps you from growing. It stunts you. Let's be honest, if you knew it and it is in every fiber of your soul, then that would make you move.

Saying "I know that" is the same as saying "I don't know," unless it's followed with concrete action. If you got your credit card bill, and you saw charges on it that you didn't make, you wouldn't just say, "Huh. That's strange. I know I didn't order a life-size sculpture of Beyoncé made entirely out of candy corn. I wonder if the UPS man will need me to be home to sign for it?" No! Your brain would kick up a fuss along the lines of "You aren't going to accept that delivery, are you? Call the credit card company and stop that order before you are stuck with candy corn Beyoncé!"

You are not an innocent bystander to your own life. Your thoughts and feelings matter, and what you LOVE matters. That was the purpose of our earlier exercise.

Here is my question to you: where are you going with that? What do you really *know* about the problem? Because if you truly *knew* it, as opposed to knowing *about* it, then you would be in a different position right now.

When you say "Yes, I know that I should do something, but…", what are you thinking? Knowing about something is the starting point. You have to launch from there. Just as we discussed in the previous chapters, where saying "I don't know" was a crutch that keeps people stuck, saying "I know that" can be a way of staying stuck. It's the same tool, the same pain. It's the same crap.

There is a difference between head knowing and heart knowing. The head knowing comes from the stories that you've learned and told yourself—and it could be the way of mentally keeping yourself stuck. Heart knowing comes from a place of personal engagement—you've got skin in the game, you want things to work out, but to get that, you've got to pay attention to your gut and intuition. It always knows.

Many times, when something we "know" is in our mind, we have the knowledge but have not grasped the reality or the consequences that will follow. So, we know it's something we should do, but we come up with excuses and we say we are not ready for it. I think that "I know" is a defense mechanism. "Oh, yeah, I know that. But I am not going to act on it." You might as well follow it up with, "I don't really know that. I think I know about that, but I'm not going to take action." And we already know that one of the key ingredients of getting unstuck is taking action. That is the sugar in the cookies. That is the flour in the cake. You can't make it without taking action.

Saying "I know that" is playing a small game because it's not forcing you to learn. When we finally do feel it in our hearts, I think it's usually because something has pained us. The pain got to the point where we couldn't ignore it anymore. Contrary to what you might think, it's usually not like, "Oh, I'm inspired to go out and conquer this mountain, once and for all!" It's more like the person who says, "Yeah, I know I shouldn't eat this, but c'mon, it's a party." If you are trying to lose weight or you're watching your cholesterol or your diabetes, you can ignore your health and say, "I know I shouldn't, but…" and choose to eat unhealthily and avoid exercise.

But then, when it hits a crisis point, like hospitalization, you are confronted with the ugly truth: you can't ignore it anymore. Then your "head knowledge" is painful and moves into a place that gets so uncomfortable that you will start doing what you have to do. The best thing we can do for ourselves is to deal with these things before we hit the crisis stage.

People can give you advice all day long, but until you get personally uncomfortable, or personally hurt, you are probably not going to follow it.

I love this truth: there's a difference between knowing something and knowing about something.

True knowing is actually part of you. It is not something that you reach for outside of you. On a personal level, you don't really know everything. We must always keep learning. We just have to keep learning. It's fun to say, "Yup, I know. I know a lot about that, but I am learning more and more every day."

Watch Out for the Know-It-All

Have you ever met someone who knows a little bit about everything? (At least *they* think so!) They "know," but they couldn't teach you anything in depth about one single topic. True knowing means that you become a student of that subject. You practice it every day. It becomes part of you and is your daily curriculum. That's the difference between knowing something and knowing about something.

Think about where you have been stuck in your life. You might find there are ways you have been fooling yourself into thinking that you have true knowing. Your ego likes to tell you, "I know all that." That goes right back to the beginning: you think you know the ocean because you put your toes in the foam at the beach. You can always go deeper.

I offer a course that I've taught over nineteen times. It's designed so that you listen to CDs with a lot of storytelling. The stories are beautiful and inspiring. They work because storytelling is one of the greatest ways to learn. You hear stories and see pictures in your mind. You put the CDs on and you relate those stories to yourself. Afterward, you do work in a workbook, and different things get triggered when you write. Deeper clarity and greater insight come out when you write; it's a process that is similar to talking with a coach. People hear themselves, and they say, "Oh, I didn't realize that was inside me."

So, I say the same things in the course every time I teach it, and I have people that have taken this course with me multiple times. I tell them: you are going to hear things differently. It's not that the materials change, it's that *you* have changed. As you change, your perception changes, and you understand things differently.

You come to a deeper knowing. The first time I hear something, I think, "Okay, I get it." Then I hear the exact same message again, and I think, "Okay, I *really* get it." And then I hear the same message yet again, and I think, "Oh, no, *now* I really get it." This goes on to the point where I realize that I'm never going to reach 100 percent—it's always going to get deeper and newer to me. The message is going to land on me differently the more often I dive into the same topic.

Consider the woman who has been reading the Bible for over thirty years. She has read it through from cover to cover, at least ten times. Yet she continues to read it almost every single day and still finds things that she is learning. She might have read a particular scripture verse many, many times before, but today was the day that it came alive to her, with a perfect application for her life. That's how you experience deeper knowing: you become an expert in it. The thing is the material may not change; the lesson may not change—*you are changing*. Therefore, it is going to be received on a different level. It's going to speak to you differently.

True knowing gets you unstuck because it's an action. True knowing is leaning in and learning. Keep learning and you will be changed. You won't be able to stay stuck when that happens. Recognizing that you don't "know it all" is one of the ways of being open to life's experiences and taking action. Feed your mind and watch the possibilities grow! And if someone is trying to help you, don't you dare say, "Yeah, I know that."

Faith in Action

Faith is another component of true knowing. As you grow deeper in knowledge, you will find there's more security in it. You grow confident in your knowledge and abilities, and you can lean toward faith rather than fear. Many times, we are stuck because we are afraid.

We've all said, "Yeah, I know, I shouldn't eat that" and gone ahead and scarfed down that pizza. Think about this: the more you say, the more you live into. If you say you know what the right choice is, but you are doing the opposite anyway, what are doing to yourself? You are hurting yourself! You are sabotaging yourself. You're staying stuck. So, what is the solution to that?

The solution is to listen, step toward it, and lean in. Learn a little more every day. Take imperfect actions. You experience it, you take more imperfect actions, but get unstuck in the process.

Practice True Knowing Today

Open yourself up to learn. Get really curious about something to act on. Learn more about the thing that is keeping you stuck—you aren't the first person to ever have this problem, I guarantee it. Ask around: who else has had this problem? How did they solve it? You don't have to do this in isolation.

Keep having faith that you can get unstuck. It's faith to believe that there is a solution. Look for encouragement and inspiration. What can I do to have a deeper understanding of this? What can I do to move in the direction of that goal? What can I do to change my perception of this or my perspective to broaden it? You have to decide that there's more to do. And then you take action in faith, not out of fear. Don't chicken out, because you can't have both, right? Pick one: faith or fear.

So, the good news is: there's an answer. There are probably a million answers. Sometimes, that answer presents itself when you are ready to listen. Like they say, "The teacher appears when the student is ready." All it takes is a change in perspective. The teacher has always been there.

There have been many times that I've bought a book, started it, got through about the first ten pages, and said, "Yeah, right." I put it on the bookshelf and forgot about it. Then, ten years later, I look at that bookshelf again and that book practically leaps out at me and jumps into my hand! I start reading it again, and it's the perfect book at the perfect time.

Earlier, I shared my story of growing up in an alcoholic home and my abandonment. At some point, I remember someone giving me an Al-Anon book about families of alcoholics. I looked at it and thought, "Blah, blah, blah." It was my crazy mom—that was the problem. Alcoholism in my family is not what messed me up as a kid; it was my mom.

I remember reading it and just thinking, "Ugh. It's a twelve-step program." The first step, I believe, is the same as in all of the AA-based programs: admitting. But it didn't do anything for me. I just thought, "This is such crap." It's like a bunch of victims running around feeling sorry for themselves. That was the state I was in: "I know this stuff already." (You see? I thought I "knew" it all!)

Then, of course, I had the great opportunity to marry my very own alcoholic and have this really tough life until I decided to make that change. I went to a Co-Dependents Anonymous meeting and I read that exact same first step, which said we were powerless over alcohol and its effects…and I bawled my eyes out. It hit me.

I did not benefit from the book at first because I had to be ready. (Hopefully, you are ready right now.) The way to get ready is you just keep going back at it until you come to the knowledge that you will *never* know it *all*.

The first step is just understanding that: know that you don't and you won't know it all. You never will know it all. The day you "knew it all", you were stuck. You were so stuck that you might as well have just curled up into a ball, you were so stuck. But you are ready to move forward, right? You've spent enough time in that place of stuckness that you are tired of knowing it all. Today, you can say, "I am going to go deeper because I don't know it all."

And that sounds great.

Chapter 8
THE POWER OF BELIEF

We are born believing.
A man bears beliefs as a tree bears apples.
Ralph Waldo Emerson

Don't tighten up on me here, okay? I know some of you reading this will be saying, "Whoa, pump those brakes. I don't do 'religious', Sam." Don't freak out.

Everybody believes in things. Every one of us. Whether you are an atheist or if you practice your faith regularly in whatever form of worship floats your boat, you have several beliefs that you hold strongly. You might believe that your soulmate is out there, somewhere. You might believe that avocado toast is overrated. You are beginning to believe that there is a way to get unstuck because you're holding this book. If you have traveled on an airplane, you believed that you would defy gravity and fly to your destination.

Belief is a frequency and a vibration. Our thoughts vibrate at higher and lower frequencies, depending on how positive or negative they are. When you think, "This is the way it is," you are expressing a powerful belief. The Grand Overall Designer—this G.O.D. I keep talking about, this Spirit, this energy—is not a sucker. You can't sit there and say, "I really believe that I could be happy," when your underlying current and vibration is "This is bullshit, I can't do this." It won't work.

When you get right down to it, we are, at our very essence, energy. (That is fact, that is science, baby.) If we believe that thoughts are real things (which they are), then to move from our stuck-ness, we have to make a shift. We must start believing that it's possible.

So far, we've talked about how you don't have to believe in this 100 percent to begin acting for change. But you *do* have to grab onto the piece you *can* believe in. And we build on that. When you can believe in "I can feel better," or "I can get over this break-up," or "I'm not giving up this time," or whatever it is—when you can believe, then it's possible. Then you will begin to see it working in your life. Start by just paying attention to your thoughts. You must pay attention to them. For instance, let's say we are talking about financial stuck-ness and you want to earn $100,000 this year, but you have never made more than $25,000. So, you write down your vision and read it, and this is your new story: "I'm so happy and grateful I made $100,000 this year." But just as often as you tell your new story, there's this little voice inside of you saying, "Ha, ha I don't think so. How am I going to ever do that?!" Can you tell that having competing teams in your head is not moving you forward? You need to change the vision.

I'm not saying, "Don't dream big," but if you write something that you can't actually energize, it's just an exercise in futility. It isn't a vision if you can't see yourself doing it! As a coach, I would say to you, "What can you get behind? What can you believe in?" You might respond, "Well, the most money I've ever made is $25,000. I believe that I could double that." All right! Let's start with that. We can use the positive energy of the belief, "I could make $50,000," instead of getting further stuck by tapping into the negative, lower-frequency energy of the belief that says,

"Yeah, right. As if. Planning on making $100,000? I may as well plan on making one million!"

It's not just reading your "LOVEs" or your new story over and over that helps. You must also find where your *ability to believe* lies. You have to energize it and build up this ability to be able to believe greater and greater things. If you don't believe it, you are energizing non-belief, which will bring your frequency down.

Why is belief the key ingredient to successful living? Purposeful, intentional belief gives you forward momentum. You can't get that from a haphazard collection of assumptions. Having a purpose keeps your eyes on the horizon and your feet moving toward the life you LOVE. It's what makes you present.

You get to recognize your own growth, your own manifestation and your skills. The day will come when you realize, "Holy crap! I *did* believe in this. I *did* energize this. I took steps every day to get here." It will take action, for sure—you can't just cross your fingers, hope that it is going to all work out, and sit locked in a closet. That's going to produce crossing your fingers locked in a closet with hope energy, which is WEAK compared to belief energy. But when you put belief energy behind those thoughts, that's when you can actually look back and say, "Whoa, I did create that." That's the successful part of belief. Our confidence and our ability to create grows and taking responsibility for those things plays a large role in our success.

So, how do you make your belief grow? You don't want to be stuck where you are, making $25,000, so you believe you can make $50,000. You still want that $100,000, but before you can believe in that reality, you need to "have a few wins" under your belt. It's much easier to believe in increments than to take on the whole enchilada in one shot.

After writing down your vision, go further and make your own vision board. I am a big fan of vision boards, and I actually stare at my own regularly. In the early days of doing this process, I read my vision every day. I was like, "ooh, I know what it says. Great." When you restate it every day, until one day you will recognize, "Holy shit, this works, I got that!"

And, most probably, it will come as a surprise to you. Because the truth of the matter is that many people won't read their new story or look at their vision board every day.

In fact, unless I remind them, after about the first month or so, my clients won't even read their story every week. This can make it seem as though you aren't making the progress you were in the beginning. But you will get a better sense of the strides you've made if you track your progress. Don't get hung up on whether you saw a big change in a single day or a single week. Think of tracking your progress like stringing beads on a necklace: on the days you have a major success, you have a big sparkly bead; other times, you might have a bunch of smaller beads strung together that represent the regular, consistent effort you put in every day.

You can set a reminder on your phone or choose a recurring date on your calendar devoted to reflection time. Get your vision board out and reflect. Another way you can get help is to hire a coach. The benefit of having a coach is having someone to keep you accountable. It's much easier to blow off an alert on your phone than to duck out on an appointment with your coach!

I do regular reviews with my clients. For example, I ask them to read their vision from six months ago, and I am able to offer a fresh perspective because I have this beautiful seat where I can look at their life without having my perspective clouded by being in their life. Many times, my clients don't give themselves credit for their growth and accomplishments. They are used to playing small and being in their stuck story. I will say, "Let's look at your vision that you gave me, that we wrote six months ago." It's always amazing to see what they have accomplished. They say things like, "Oh my God, I didn't even realize that I had come this far." When you energize your vision, it's astonishing how G.O.D., Spirit, and the Universe jumps on board with you.

Remember the client we talked about earlier who wanted to design homes? She wanted to get into big renovation designs: adding rooms, moving walls, and things like that. So, we really clarified that vision. Not long after that, though, we had a massive hurricane and it destroyed the real estate office where she worked. She couldn't go in to do her job because the building had been so badly damaged that repairs were estimated to take six months. So, she was unemployed while they were rebuilding it.

Then, out of the blue, a friend called her and asked if she would come and work in their design furniture store. Intriguing. Unsolicited, she gets an invitation that was part of her vision. She gets to work with fabrics, and she gets to work with design. G.O.D., Spirit, and Universe tapped her friend on the shoulder and told her to make the call. She didn't choose the *how*, but her belief, her vision, was manifested.

Here is another example of how G.O.D., Spirit, and Universe worked in my life. A few months ago, I was sitting at home, looking at my vision board where it said, "My kitchen is exactly how I want it." I had a clear picture of how my dream kitchen would look like, but I had been putting it off. Just prior to taking my summer sabbatical, I reached out to my carpenter and said, "Hey, when I get back, I want to put new countertops in my kitchen and extend the island. So, I just want you to be prepared for that."

He nodded his head and said, "Yep, for sure. We can start when you get back."

When I got back home, my cabinets were infested with termites.

AAAAGGHHH!!! DISASTER!... Or was it?

Guess what? I am going to get my dream kitchen because now I *have* to. That's not how I would have planned it. In my mind, I was just talking about refurbishing and adding some new countertops. But my true dream kitchen, which is what I have in my vision, is the current kitchen that is being built. I put my dream kitchen out there and G.O.D., Spirit, and Universe said, "Your wish is my command."

I was going to be conservative and just refurbish my cabinets, but G.O.D., Spirit, and Universe saw right through that mess. "Really, Sam? You're not giving yourself that dream kitchen? You were just going to nickel and dime yourself and call it 'good enough'?!? Nuh-uh, I don't work that way." The Universe heard me when I said, "dream kitchen." The Universe heard me when I said, "exactly as I wanted." My friends, "good enough" is nice, but I am done with settling for "good enough." I am willing to wait and believe that LOVE is on the way. The Universe has bigger plans than you or I do. If you are believing for a dream, then BELIEVE IT*!*

It's amazing how we arrive at these situations. I've always said, "The *how* is none of your business; it's the *what*. What would you love? What can you do today in the direction of creating, manifesting, and getting what you love?"

G.O.D., Spirit, and Universe have perfect hearing and want to supply you with what you want, but you will get exactly what you asked for, as long as you truly believe it.

Your belief matters a great deal because you will receive what you believed you are worthy of. I was going to shrink my vision to make it fit what I believe I deserved. But like I said before, G.O.D., Spirit, and Universe have bigger and better plans than we do and want to partner with you! My order was filled, but just not how I thought it was going to go.

Nowhere in my plans would I have met my husband. I never wrote, "I am going to meet a Canadian in Canada, move there, and become Canadian." That I couldn't have planned—that's THE HOW— I wouldn't have written that as a story.

Manifesting really does work. It does not always unfold the way you imagine it happening, but when you look back, you think, "Holy shit, this stuff works."

You might be wondering if this sounds a little too easy: "just believe" sounds a little too good to be true. Well, it *is* true that believing will have you receiving, but you're still wise to be cautious (scratch that, *intentional*) about *what* you believe.

You need to know that there are some risks in putting your belief, your thought energy, into lower energy stories. As I mentioned earlier, it's important that you be careful what you wish for. The Universe is a perfect vibrational match to you. If you want to know where your thoughts are, where your beliefs are taking you, then look at your life. Your life is the end result of your thinking. It is the result of your vibrations and of your manifestations.

We manifest good and bad all the time; that's what we do. We create our realities. We are completely responsible for our perceptions, which create our beliefs. Ultimately, our beliefs create our realities. We all know a guy who says, "I can never find a girlfriend. Women don't want to talk with me, or they tell me that they would rather just be friends." Or a woman who says, "Guys won't like me because I'm overweight. I can't fall in love until I am in perfect shape." Whatever you speak is your truth. In these examples, they are tapping into the dangerous side of belief.

Here's the thing: if you put energy into the low-vibration thoughts, such as "I am not loveable," then G.O.D., Spirit, and Universe scratch their metaphorical heads and sigh, "Okay, if that's really what you want…Your wish is my command."

If that's your belief, you are going to get more of it. Your thoughts are like seeds. No one would expect to get watermelons if they planted corn. Undermining your stories with negative, low-frequency thoughts will grow into a bumper crop of NOT ITs. You made that with your beliefs.

Going back to my mom, she was married *seven* times. S E V E N (It still blows my mind.) And although my mom was not an alcoholic, she married them. There was no thread, but she was a magnet for alcoholic abusers because she would always say, "What I don't want is somebody who…" She was full of *what she didn't want*. She always energized what she didn't want. So, the Universe said, "Okay, I am getting a really strong message about alcoholic abusers. If that's what you really want…"

You may remember this from *The Secret*: don't use the word "don't" in your visualization. We know further that we can't ignore the NOT ITs in our lives.

Remember the example I gave you about picturing the Eiffel Tower? We are going to reframe the negative because G.O.D., Spirit, and Universe do not hear "don't." For example, if I say to you, "I am thinking about an animal that lives in Africa. It has four legs, giant floppy ears, and a long trunk, lives in groups, and has great hearing." But then I restrict you by saying, "Don't think about elephants. Whatever you do, don't picture a huge, adorable, grey creature that trumpets and flies around a circus tent. Oh, yeah, there was also one in a famous Disney movie." Were you thinking about *Dumbo* just now? That's the point. "Don't" doesn't work.

The Universe just hears the vibration that you are putting out. When you have low-level vibrations like, "Poor me, this always happens to me. I always end up with assholes," the vibration is "This woman doesn't like nice guys." Whatever is the strongest message is going to get the most action.

The intensity of the emotion behind any thought, any desire, is crucial. It's like faith and fear. They cannot co-exist; you must pick one. You can't have both.

Chapter 9
YOU CAN START RIGHT NOW

The secret of getting ahead is getting started.
Mark Twain

Anybody who has experienced a physical transformation knows that whether it's weight loss or building muscle, change is gradual. You may know it from looking at the mirror, or the feedback we get from stepping on a scale; initially, the changes we are making are sometimes hard to see at first. When we really get powerful feedback is when someone hasn't seen us in six months, and their mind is blown. "Oh my God, you look amazing!" they'll say. That feels good! Then you can look at yourself with their eyes and truly appreciate the progress you have made. Maybe you haven't noticed the baby steps that you are making, but they are accumulating, and, along the way, you are feeling much better.

I lost forty pounds more than two years ago. I had been sort of trying to lose weight since my last child, and then it just started piling on at age forty-five. I quit smoking, I started working from home, and my hormones started playing a part—it was the perfect storm for gaining weight.

I am telling you, I was really trying hard to get the weight off. I was eating properly, exercising regularly, you know, all the usual stuff. What happened then was I stopped gaining weight, which is good. At least I stopped going in the wrong direction with all my hard work. But the truth is that even today, two years later, people say, "You just look so great." I didn't gain weight overnight. It didn't come off the first time I tried, and it didn't even come off the second time I tried, or what felt like the 100th time I tried. But it did come off when I found a diet, or better, *a lifestyle change*, that resonated with me. I became committed, got consistent, and stuck with it. This is true for you, too, in an emotional or mental transformation.

It is the ride. You get to feel a little bit better every day when you are on the right path. But it's also like dancing the cha-cha: it is two steps forward, and one step back sometimes. Don't beat yourself up if you took a step back. Big deal! Next time you get on the dance floor, take the two-step-forward part.

If you are trying to improve your health for the first time (or whatever area of growth you are currently working on) and you are making a big change, a crucial concept that you must internalize is that your progress is not a straight line. Rather, you should tell yourself, "Oh, it's supposed to be like this. I'm not doing it wrong just because I've had a step back here." You can give yourself a pat on the back because your path looks exactly like it's supposed to look. We are making a spiritual, emotional, and mental transformation here.

The contrast between personal and physical transformation is not so different. Have you ever heard someone say, "Oh well, I had wine and cheese last night, so I will start my diet on Monday"? And what do they do next? Basically, they pound down as much wine and cheese as possible until they get to Monday. You don't wait until Monday; that's a setup. It's a game. It's a way of failing.

When you do have a slip-up—oh, and you will, it's part of your role as a card-carrying member of humanity—when that happens, you don't lie down and give up. You now say, "Oh well, shit happens, this is just what it looks like as it is working out." *Do not* say, "I slipped, I will start again on Monday." Draw the line, *right there and then*, and start again. You need to realize that failure is feedback. It is information to be used in future encounters, choices, and decisions. Failure is simply data. Use it for your own good!

Learning is knowing that to move forward, we are going to take a step back every once in a while. That's growth, that's progress, and that's paradigms trying to seduce you. Whatever causes it, just expect it to happen and know that the next best move is your next step forward. That's it, keep moving no matter what. Just remember that there is no better time than NOW to make your change.

Get a PIMP

What else can you do beyond what we have already done with "what we LOVE" and writing our story about everything we LOVE as if we already have it. You can always get a PIMP. It's fun. If you haven't figured something out about me yet, I love to have fun. I love it.

[Crickets chirp in the distance.]

Have I told you about a PIMP before? A P.I.M.P. is a Powerful, Important, Morning Practice. Think about how you can begin your own powerful, important, morning practice.

Now, truthfully, you can do it at night too, but that doesn't rhyme. It would be hard to say. So, I am going to go ahead and share with you what I've shared with other readers in the past. I used to make up a journal for people, and it was downloaded thousands of times. Pick up your own copy of P.I.M.P. at *www.adesignedlifellc.com*

In part of the journal, I introduce the idea that powerful routines produce powerful results. You will want to design your personal P.I.M.P. tool kit customized to give you the most benefit. There are many "right" ways of achieving your right thing, not just one way of doing things to get your desired result. So, I love to give people this tool kit. You decide which is going to work best for you. I am not going to tell you that you must do nine things in your Powerful, Important, Morning Practice, even though I might give you nine suggestions here. I want you to pick two or three and see what tastes good to you. It's like a menu.

P.I.M.P. "Soul Food" Menu

&&&

Gratitude, Meditation

&

Breathing Exercises

&

Intention and Affirmations

&

Visualization, Journaling

&&&

Gratitude

> *If you are not grateful for all that you already have, what makes you think you would be happier with more?*
> **Roy T. Bennett,** *The Light in the Heart*

In practicing gratitude, I encourage you to write at least five things you have in your life that you are grateful for. I encourage you to start with listing just five different things. Then, the next morning, read the list of the five you have and add one more. Do this every day for thirty days, but, here's the kicker, you cannot repeat anything that's already on the list. Whenever you read the list, you add a new gratitude. Read the list, add a new gratitude. This is not an exercise to just do and get over with, it is truly transformational. You are going to have to start digging deep on Day Twenty and that, my friend, is when the magic starts to happen. When I first started this practice, I would say, "I am so grateful for my cozy bed because my mornings are where I have my coffee in bed." It was the best thing ever. I really do enjoy that part of my day. When I kept using that as one of my go-to lines, though, it became too common and it stopped lifting my vibration.

The goal for this exercise is to bring you to fully realize your abundance: "Oh, I already have so much. I am so grateful that I am waking up to the smell of coffee brewing downstairs. I am so grateful that I even woke up this morning. I am so grateful that my towels are clean. I am so grateful that the heat is on in the bathroom. I am so grateful I have a car to get into today. I am so grateful I get to take the bus to work and don't have to be stuck in traffic." There are so many great things that we can look at and be happy about.

Meditation

I find that meditation is essential for most people's mental well-being and clarity. Meditation is the practice of observing your thoughts and feelings to gain perspective. It's not a competition, and it isn't judgment. I used to suck at meditating. Can you start with meditating for a minute? Can you do three minutes? I don't care how long someone meditates. If it's three minutes or three hours, that's up to you.

Just trust that, by quieting that monkey mind, there's some cool universal intelligence working within you at that moment. Just a few minutes of stillness is a gift that only you can give yourself. That's all you have to know. But it's about you learning to quiet your monkey mind and just be.

If people tell me, "I don't know how to meditate," I suggest they look it up, Google it, and start to explore. Meditating is actually not that hard, once your mind starts to wander (or in other words, SQUIRREL!) You just focus back on your breathing. Three minutes of meditation for me is an eternity, and I am not exaggerating. I just run with a high mind. But that's my personal practice—it's not a competition.

Breathing Exercises

This is the part of my meditation to get deep rejuvenating oxygen floating into my lungs and brain. I always recommend that people put both feet on the floor. Be grounded, expand those lungs as big as possible, and oxygenate.

HealthLinkBC (www.healthlinkbc.ca/health-topics) gives an excellent breathing exercise that you can try at home:

Belly breathing

Belly breathing is easy to do and very relaxing. Try this basic exercise anytime you need to relax or relieve stress.

1. Sit or lie flat in a comfortable position.
2. Put one hand on your belly just below your ribs and the other hand on your chest.
3. Take a deep breath in through your nose, and let your belly push your hand out. Your chest should not move.
4. Breathe out through pursed lips as if you were whistling. Feel the hand on your belly go in and use it to push all the air out.
5. Do this breathing three to ten times. Take your time with each breath.
6. Notice how you feel at the end of the exercise.

Intention and Affirmation

There is a saying: where you place your *attention* becomes your *intention*.

Your intention is your message to Source, to the Universe, and to G.O.D. It is your vibration for the day or start of the day, at the very least. Intention is married to affirmation. They date, they hang out.

You create intentions by using an "I am" statement or something similar. You could go back and grab your vision board and write:

Today I am _____.

Today I will _____.

Today is _____.

Let me marry intention to affirmation, so that you see how they work together.

With affirmations, we choose words that inspire us, and they will accurately state our deepest heartfelt desires. There is a specific formula to use when creating affirmations: use positive language in the present tense and frame these statements as facts. Affirmations are not wishes; that's why they are called *affirm*ations. We aren't crossing our fingers as in "I wish", or "I hope." Affirmations are the "I AM's" and "I have" thoughts vibrating at the level you know is yours. You know it's yours, so, you can start an affirmation like this:

"I am so happy and grateful that I am…"

"I am so happy and grateful that I have…"

I have a few personal favorites from some of the great thinkers of our time. One's from Bob Proctor, one's from Napoleon Hill, and the other one is Tony Robbins.

1. *I am so happy and grateful now that money is coming to me in increasing amounts on a continuous basis through multiple sources.* **-Bob Proctor**

2. *Life is full of love and I find it everywhere I go.* **-Samantha Buckley Hugessen**

3. *I am here to help people have better lives, connections, and experiences. I am truly successful, and I make a great living doing it.* **-Napoleon Hill**

4. *I am calm and patient with people.* **-Samantha Buckley Hugessen**

5. *Every need, desire and goal I have is met instantaneously by infinite intelligence.* **-Tony Robbins**

Affirmations are incredible tools for increasing your positive energy, but you have to buy into them so they can work for you. You may feel silly writing and saying them at first, but that's okay. Think of the first time you tried something like driving a car, playing a sport, or learning a computer program. Initially, it's awkward and maybe seems like a lot to learn and remember to get it to flow right, but that is part of the process. Try it with an open mind and see if affirmations are a good fit for you.

It's not the word; it's the energy behind the word. Energy has a frequency or a vibration—that's the thing you have to really know, and that is why I keep repeating it throughout this book.

A thought has a frequency or a vibration; that's how it becomes a thing.

All the scientific tests where they talk badly to or bully a plant and it withers, or they talk nicely to another plant and it thrives, are examples of how the thought energy behind the words has power. Plants don't know the words "hate" or "ugly" or "love," but they sense the vibration and frequency of them. A rhododendron doesn't know the word "hate." I'm sorry, but it doesn't. (If it does, awesome, I want some of what you are having.)

So, you can sit there and say, "I'm rich. I'm nice. I'm beautiful. And gosh darn it, people like me," but if you don't believe it, none of it is going to happen. Because the energy you are putting behind it is "I don't believe this. I don't buy it. It ain't true." Good luck getting the positive energy from that! If you can't get energetically aligned with it, then forget it. Who are you conning? "Like attracts like," as the saying (or Universal law) goes.

Visualization

Then, after affirmations, we spend time visualizing. These three elements work great when they are done together. Affirmations, intentions, visualizing– creating a visualization is actually a necessary part of any affirmation or intention routine. Your mind doesn't think in verbal propositions. It thinks in images. So, if I said, "I want you to picture a tree," what do you see in your mind? Maybe a pine or a maple tree, right? If you are wishing you were somewhere warm, maybe it's a palm tree, but chances are you didn't see the word in black and white and spelled out t-r-e-e; rather, you saw the earth-grown tree. That's the creative visualization. Now here's another question to ponder: is it *real?*

Visualizing is simply using a natural function of your mind to your own advantage. It's already a natural function of your mind to think in images. When we use bright and clear moving pictures of what we really want to achieve, it helps us move our subconscious minds into that action much quicker.

Modern researchers contend that the human nervous system really can't tell the difference between a real, external experience and a visualization. For example, let's go back to the research performed on athletes in the 1970s. The test subjects were runners that were told to imagine running races in their mind while they were hooked up to medical monitoring equipment. The runners were told to be as accurate as possible, adding details like what clothes they were wearing and the sound of their feet on the gravel track as they hit their stride. What did the studies find? The athletes' bodies responded as if they were *actually running*, including increased heart rates. It didn't matter that they were lying down on a bed—actual physiological changes took place in response to the messages coming from their brains. That's the power of visualization.

In my late teens, I had a friend in her early twenties, who studied to be a court reporter. She studied hard and found her first job.

It took a long time of studying and practice for her and after she finally got the job that she had been working toward all this time, she came home sobbing. She was a mess, crying, "I don't know what I am going to do! It was a horrible experience!"

The problem was not the act of typing transcripts, but the trial itself, which was about a horrible criminal act. She was completely immersed in what was going on in the court and the problem was that she was internalizing it. As the witnesses told the story, she was seeing it happen because her mind painted the picture in front of her. Her mind's ability to visualize was recreating the crime in her head.

The advice I gave her years ago to teach her how to distance herself from the crime was to see it in black and white as though she was watching an old movie or reading a newspaper. Otherwise, the stories that she would hear as a court reporter would be too painful to experience, even second-hand. Using this technique to dull the experience became a useful strategy that allowed her to perform her job effectively.

That's how powerful mental imagery can be. Put it on, feel it, smell it, and taste it. These are all tools I use to help people to really see their dream. Spending time visualizing is paramount. I would tell every single person, if this is their first time, to start with a sample P.I.M.P. menu. I would recommend that their first tools to explore would be to practice gratitude and spend time visualizing daily. Walk through your day in your mind, really working it out beautifully and in detail.

One way to get the most out of your visualization practice would be to pair it up with your vision board to read and refine your vision daily. That is a very Powerful, Important, Morning Practice: reading the written vision. Put it on, see yourself in that role, and ask, "What can I do today, in the direction of …?" There's always a thing to do.

Many times, people aren't going to do it. It's no surprise to me and it's okay. I understand. You are not going to be perfect at this. Sometimes you might wake up and say, "What can I do today?" and nothing comes to mind. Well, read your vision, there's a thing you can do. I promise it will show up, and it will propel you. It will do something for you.

I have one more. Are you ready?

Journaling

You ink it. You just don't think it. There is something very powerful in writing. There's a program in Asia that works with dementia patients. It gets them to write about their experience and, while it's not a cure, they are finding that the patients' comprehension, memory, and understanding has improved. The connection to the information deepens greatly by writing.

When we are journaling as a P.I.M.P., we are *not* talking about typing on a computer. It should be the act of physically picking up a piece of paper and pen (or a journal) and writing. *Don't just think it, ink it.*

If you decide to journal as one of your selections from the P.I.M.P. menu, give yourself permission to write whatever comes to mind without censoring yourself. Write your thoughts, your dreams, and your goals. Write out your learning points, the easy lessons, and the harder ones to swallow. Write them down. It's fine to write something like, "Okay, that sucked, but..." Here's the good news: inking it takes the harder lessons and gives you the distance you need to assess your situation differently.

You will get the most benefit from this process if you add a second step: review. You just write whatever flows from you, and then you review it once some time has passed-- on a quarterly basis, for example. Go back and look what you wrote for the last few months. I would love for people to do it monthly, but you can decide what works best for you. Decide on a regular review date and put it on the calendar; make an alert.

But, what do you do if you stumble or screw up?

You could stumble. You can sabotage yourself at times. You can slip "or cha-cha". You can find that there will be points in your journey where you stumble. It goes back to a whole lifetime of experiences leading up to where you are now. Be a little kinder with yourself. Recognize that if you ski down the hill and you never fall, you are not pushing yourself, you are not getting better, or taking any risks. You played it way too safe. You are *supposed* to fall; that's how you learn.

My husband was a ski instructor growing up. When we first started dating, I was a "ski-a-couple-of-times-a-year" girl. My style was just "ski fast and down the hill." When I first started really skiing with him, I remember saying, "Yay, I didn't fall." He said, "That's not it. You actually kind of want to fall when you are learning. Otherwise, you're not pushing the boundaries. You are not stretching and getting better."

If you don't stumble, you won't know what to do when a problem does crop up. You won't know how to fall. Learn how to fall; it's fine. And then you learn how to get back up. You don't lay there waiting for the snow plow to go over you, or the groomer to take you out. (Or the snow to melt so that you can walk down the hill. "Yo, I will see you in April!")

You learn to get up. You are supposed to push up against things that challenge you. That's growth, my friend. You have to recognize the situation and ask yourself, "Is this real or is this my saboteur kicking in?" Either way, get up. It's the only way it's going to work. You can't beat the saboteur by sitting there, and you can't get down the hill by sitting there. You have to get up and take action.

I have a client who constantly tells me that the greatest gift I give her is teaching her about ACTION. She is adorable and has made action a fun mantra for herself: *Action is the magic pill.* ACTION IS THE MAGIC PILL. Take a step, and I promise that you will feel better.

I know I make it sound easy because it is. The same will power is used in achieving your greater good as it is in sabotaging yourself. It's the same will. Will is will. That's all I am saying. People make this so much harder than it really is, they really, really do.

And I am one of them.

I smoked for almost thirty-five years. Yes, I know, gross. I started when I was twelve. If you think I haven't told myself every story, every excuse, and every reason why I smoked, you'd be wrong. C'mon! Of course, I did!

I quit smoking in 2012, and I had stopped before that when I was pregnant, of course, because my kids' lives meant so much more than my own life clearly at that time. I would do it for them, but I wouldn't do it for me because I had conned myself into thinking that I loved smoking. For you, it might be kind of like I love cookies. I love chaos in my life.

No, you don't; you are just comfortable in the stuck place you have been for so long. We are going to get you comfortable in the unstuck place of action and flow instead. You will feel a lot better when you write a new story. Let your journal and vision guide you out of that place.

Consistency

It's a habit. You do things until they become your norm, like anything else you have learned. Change a habit to make it consistent. It's always going to be uncomfortable in the beginning. Don't let that discourage you. Think of it like you are making deposits in a bank account called "MY AWESOME LIFE".

Practice makes perfect and consistency is the key. It's creating your new normal, replacing your old paradigms, and replacing your old habits. As I said before, paradigms are sneaky little bitches. They will come up and convince you of things. If you have consistent structures, plans, and actions in your life—like consistently meditating, consistency with your affirmations, and consistently visualizing—then it makes it a lot harder for those nasty little old habits and paradigms to get in.

It's like the person who quit smoking, drinking, and eating junk and then started again after five years. Or the person who quit drinking. The guy who used to religiously go to the gym and stopped. The woman who gave up carbs and started eating pizza and pasta again. It's a life-long practice. This is a life-long change and it becomes your new normal as long as you continue with the new habits. You have heard it said before: you are either on a diet or you are making a lifelong life-style change. Which is it?

Anthony Robbins talks about the idea that you have to *practice* to become perfect. I remember reading this about him many years ago. As he began his career in public speaking, he just started scheduling speaking engagements as often as he could because people told him it would take years to get good at it. He thought, "What if I don't have that kind of time? What if I speed that up? Rather than just doing a speaking engagement twice a month, what if I did it twice a week?" Now he is world famous for public speaking. You *are* going to get good at it—if you practice.

If you keep at it, keep practicing, it's going to get easy. It's going to become normal. A child doesn't learn to walk by falling down and thinking, "Yeah, I guess I'm just not meant to walk.

I will just sit here, stuck in this poopy diaper forever." They get back up and do it again and again until they are traversing the household furniture with reckless abandon. And you will too! That's the idea of consistency. The more you do it, the more it becomes second nature.

How many times have you driven home from someplace and not even remembered how you got there? (I am not saying you were drunk.) Once you have driven the route so many times, it becomes second nature and you drive on autopilot. Same old, same old with what I am sharing with you here. However, getting that comfortable here could also be to your detriment because you might think, "I'm cured! I will never slip again."

This is why we check in and track our progress with our visions. Because when you read them, it brings you back to the center. (Which is why visions are so cool!) You will find yourself saying, "I forgot I did that. Oh my God, I already have that. That's amazing. I didn't even realize I had this in my vision, and here it is in my life!" I hear it every day. You will, too, with consistent practice of your own P.I.M.P.

CHAPTER 10
THE KEY TO LIFE: GRATITUDE

> *Happiness cannot be traveled to, owned, earned, worn or consumed. Happiness is the spiritual experience of living every minute with love, grace, and gratitude.*
> **Denis Waitley**

I'm super grateful.

It's amazing how, when you shift your thinking, it shifts your energy and shifts your outcome. It's crazy. Gratitude is the key to life. It has a neutralizing power on negativity and anxiety. When you focus on being grateful, you are very present and experiencing life in the way you were meant to do.

Gratitude is a shift in me. That's the only thing that I can control. That's the only thing that we can control. It's a shift in us. A recent Harvard Medical School study describes it this way: "Gratitude is a thankful appreciation for what an individual receives, whether tangible or intangible." When people acknowledge the goodness in their lives, they begin to "recognize that the source of that goodness lies at least partially outside themselves. Research shows that people who practice gratitude consistently experience greater happiness than those who do not" (*https://www.health.harvard.edu/healthbeat/giving-thanks-can-make-you-happier*). That alone should sell you on trying this!

Gratitude helps people to practice thinking positively. The more time they spend reliving good moments, the more it acts like an injection that helps them become more resilient when they go through life's challenges. (It's a "booster shot" for your mind!) Gratitude can also pump up your relationships. It strengthens and connects people on a deeper level, whether it is a romantic relationship, friendship, or professional relationship.

Research on Gratitude

There is growing research to support the idea that gratitude helps with mental health. According to recent psychological studies, Dr. Robert A. Emmons, (University of California, Davis), and Dr. Michael E. McCullough (University of Miami), have specialized their research on how practicing gratitude in everyday life can benefit your health. One study had all the participants write a few sentences each week, focusing on how they were feeling about particular topics.

Group One practiced gratitude by writing about how they were grateful for various things that had occurred during the week. Group Two took the opposite approach: they were encouraged to complain and write about little things that had irritated or frustrated them throughout the week. The control group wrote about events that had affected them (with no emphasis on them being positive or negative).

Ten weeks later, participants from Group One ("Team Gratitude") were more optimistic and felt better about their lives. Surprisingly, the benefits carried beyond mental health into physical health. Team Gratitude exercised more often and had fewer doctors' visits than those who were in Team "Attitude",

Dr. Martin E. P. Seligman, (University of Pennsylvania), created another type of gratitude test, Participants were asked to write a letter of gratitude to someone in their life whom they felt had never been properly thanked for his or her kindness. Then, the letter writers were asked to personally deliver their thank-you notes. After connecting with their benefactors, participants immediately experienced a huge increase in their happiness scores. This particular exercise had a huge impact, with mental health benefits lasting for a month. (Healthbeat 2014)

Wow! Do you want that kind of boost? Get writing!

Of course, in studies such as these, you can't really prove cause and effect. But most of the studies published on this topic support an association between gratitude and an individual's well-being.

So, how can you begin to explore your own gratitude practice?

Two Types of Gratitude

It may be that you haven't thought of gratitude as a practice beyond Thanksgiving Day. There's being grateful for *stuff*; for example, I'm grateful for my bed or a roof over my head, and I'm grateful for the first cup of coffee in the morning. This is gratitude connected to the physical world—things that we can see, taste, or touch. The second type of gratitude is connected to *concepts:* I'm grateful for my partner, or I'm grateful for friends and family (the concepts of relationship, belonging, and love); I'm grateful for God (the concept of faith). This kind of gratitude is linked to our emotions.

If I ask people, "What are you grateful for?" they almost always answer the first three: I am grateful for God, I'm grateful for my family, and I'm grateful for my health. Those three, though not necessarily in that order, are almost always the first.

Now, thinking the same, standard "roll off your tongue without really thinking or feeling deep" gratitude practice is okay, but chances are, you aren't really lifting your vibration. It's a kind of lip-service—a prepared answer that has become a habit. Although it is nice that at least you have that habit. Even saying you are grateful for anything shows that you are on a good path.

The truth is that we need to drill in our gratitude a little bit deeper. That's where the magic happens. Use the Gratitude tool from your P.I.M.P. menu to drill deeper into your own gratitude experience.

Maybe you sit in bed in the morning and you say to yourself, "I am going to do my gratitudes." At first, you just think them. You roll them around in your mind and count them off on your fingers. I'm going to encourage, as always, that you think them and that you have a portion in your personal journal reserved for your written gratitude thoughts.

Gratitude for material things is the easiest thing. Who doesn't like good stuff like a soft, warm bed, or a dinner out at a fancy restaurant? It's not a big stretch to identify good things and think fondly about the way you feel when you received these gifts. Gratitude for situations can be a lot harder. Where do you find the silver lining in a less than desirable situation? It's much harder to ask, "What in this situation am I grateful for?"

For instance, I can use something as simple as my termite-infested kitchen. My original renovation plans went awry, and then things went further downhill when the contractor quit after ripping me off for my deposit money and the workers showed up on their own time, or often not at all!

What the hell could I be grateful for in that chaos?

You have to know that I am super-orderly and maybe a smidge over the top when it comes to order. In the midst of my kitchen renovation shitshow I was in, I had to use the barbecue and microwave when I did attempt to cook and fed my kids pizza and tacos when I couldn't. Dishes were being done in the utility sink in the laundry room. The "three-week job" became a six- or seven-week job that I was now running and, frankly, I was pissed off. And, apparently, being pissed wasn't fixing the situation. In fact, it made things worse. So, I stopped. I just stopped the venom-spitting and went to gratitude. It is the quickest way I know out of a yucky state.

Let me walk you through how it went. I'm grateful that I have the resources so that I can afford to replace my kitchen. There were plenty of times in my life where termite-infested cabinets would have had to stay that way because I didn't have the money to replace them. So, I am really grateful for that. I am grateful that I work from home, so I could run the job going on downstairs and do my job in my office.

I am grateful that even though the workers were a bit too relaxed, working on their own schedule and not the one they promised me, I met some really great tradesmen that I can use in future projects. I am grateful that, at the end of all of this, I am going to have a beautiful kitchen that I am proud of, I love to cook in, and where I can bring my family and friends to share food and drinks together around the giant island. Yes, it was a sucky situation. Having everything torn up around us and not having people show up, having people quit and having to pay more money made for additional challenges. But I am truly grateful for the lesson.

> *Let us rise up and be thankful, for if we didn't learn a lot today, at least we learned a little, and if we didn't learn a little, at least we didn't get sick, and if we got sick, at least we didn't die; so, let us all be thankful.*
> **Buddha**

So, the tool that you can use in the future is that you must ask yourself: *what is the good that I can pull from this?* Where is the opportunity in this for me to experience gratitude? I gave you an idea of the stuff that I felt gratitude for: a beautiful new kitchen and lovely furnishings. But I can go beyond the *stuff* and say that I'm also grateful for the connections I made, the new plumber, electrician, and carpenter I met. What else am I grateful for? I am grateful for the lesson because I will not repeat that one again! I will get, at minimum, three references on contractors in the future, not just three bids. Lesson learned.

Right now, some of you might be saying, "Oh sure, Sam, you were grateful for the lesson and that must be nice for you in your enlightened brain, but what about the angry feeling of being ripped off? I'd have smoke coming out of my ears! How does that work in with the gratitude?"

Honestly, when it first happened, that contractor was not safe to walk down the halls of my mind! If I had a giant cartoon mallet like in a Bugs Bunny cartoon, I would have flattened him like a pancake. I was so angry that day and actually hurt because I was thinking, "I am a good person—why would somebody do that to *me*?" Make sense?

I was stuck, that's what was happening to me. The only person who was getting hurt over all of that was me. The person who was carrying the piece of coal and getting burned by being so pissed off was me. So, I decided to look at it differently. I changed my perception by stopping myself and saying, "Okay, what's the good in this?" In other words, what am I grateful for? That stopped the coal from continuing to burn me. I put the coal down.

I changed my perception and thought about how the guy *did* pay his workers a percentage of the money he took from me. So, a portion of my deposit paid them.

I think that those workers needed it more than I did. Thinking about the good that was done took the charge out of that negative thought pattern. I've always told people before you make a big decision, give it seventy-two hours. It's only three days. Just give it those three days because the whole situation may change, or your charge around it may change.

Now, here I am two weeks later, and the charge for me has passed because I put my energy into it all working out and getting done. And I am grateful for meeting these great workers and being able to afford to give them proper payment for their great work. I cut him—the problem—out of the equation. It wasn't instantaneous and I'm not going to be nominated for sainthood anytime soon, not gonna gloss over that! I am going to tell you the truth about this because you still have to deal with your feelings when these things happen, regardless of how good you are at other parts of the practice. These negative feelings need some direction.

We have facts and we have truths. I have had my struggles, just like you have had your own. I've felt like I'm waist-deep in mud and someone's backing a fresh truckload of shit to add to the pile. One thing after another kept piling up, after another, after another, and I woke up one day and said: this is not serving me.

I said, "Sam, you are in a shitty vibration, so you are just getting more of it." And guess what? The facts of the situations didn't change. My kitchen was still torn up, and the contractor was still MIA. The facts didn't change, but my truth changed.

The truth is I don't let these things ruin my peace. I am the only one suffering here. And, quite frankly, I don't prefer suffering. I prefer joy, happiness, and ease. So, I drew a line and I let it go. I said, "It's going to happen when it happens." That's the honest truth, and my level of stress has been so reduced since then. This peace is what I want for all my clients.

The Science of Happiness

There are several physicians and scientists who are studying what mental and physical benefits might be connected with gratitude. Remember earlier, when I told you about some gratitude studies? Here's one of the studies that looked at how gratitude can help improve mental health. Researchers at Indiana University focused specifically on psychotherapy patients who were seeking help with the issues of depression and anxiety.

Study participants were put into one of three groups. All three groups received counseling services, but the first group was also instructed to write one letter of gratitude to another person each week for three weeks. The second group was asked to write about their deepest thoughts and feelings about negative experiences. The third group did not do any writing activity. (They were the control group.)

Compared with the participants in Group Two, who wrote about their negative experiences, or the control group who only received counseling, the participants in Group One who wrote gratitude letters reported significantly better mental health four weeks and twelve weeks after their writing exercise ended. This suggests that gratitude writing can be beneficial not just for healthy, well-adjusted individuals, but also for those who struggle with mental health concerns. In fact, it seems, practicing gratitude on top of receiving psychological counseling carries greater benefits than counseling alone, even when that gratitude practice is brief. Gratitude can enhance healing. (Greater Good Magazine 2017)

Four Benefits of Gratitude

Disconnect from toxic emotions. The researchers analyzed the words used by participants in the two writing groups, to better understand the benefits of gratitude letter writing. They compared the percentage of positive emotion words, negative emotion words, and "we" words (first-person plural words) that participants used in their writing. Not surprisingly, those in the gratitude writing group used a higher percentage of positive emotion words and "we" words, and a lower proportion of negative emotion words, than those in the other writing group.

However, people who used more positive emotion words and more "we" words in their gratitude letters didn't necessarily have better mental health later. It was only when people used fewer negative emotion words in their letters that they were significantly more likely to report better mental health. In fact, it was the *lack of negative emotion words*—not the abundance of positive words—that explained the mental health gap between the gratitude writing group and the other writing group. THAT IS FRIGGIN' COOL SCIENCE right there, people!

Turning away from toxic emotions like resentment, bitterness, and envy lets you gain a new perspective. When you write about how grateful you are to others and how much other people have blessed your life, it becomes considerably harder for you to sit and stew on your negative experiences. Your brain doesn't like to hold two opposing thoughts!

You can still benefit from practicing gratitude, even if you don't share it. The study did not require the participants to send the letters, only to write them. Some did mail the letters, but it did not make as much difference as the act of writing the letter. This is good news if you have a message for someone who has fallen out of touch, or someone who has passed away: write the letter anyway.

Be patient. The benefits of practicing gratitude are a bit like planting a garden. You are growing something good, and that takes time. The participants in the study didn't notice much difference after a week, but they did after four weeks or more. This isn't a microwave dinner, this is soul food.

Gratitude changes your brain. I have talked about changing your wiring earlier in this book, and this study has actual physical evidence to support this. Dr. Joel Wong and Dr. Joshua Brown did this study: *Using an MRI scanner to measure brain activity while people from each group did a "pay it forward" task, the individuals were regularly given a small amount of money by a nice person, called the "benefactor." This benefactor only asked that they pass the money on to someone if they felt grateful. Our participants then decided how much of the money, if any, to pass on to a worthy cause (which was donated to a local charity).*

(Greater Good Magazine 2017)

They found that when people felt more grateful, their brain activity was distinct from brain activity related to guilt and the brain activity associated with the desire to help a cause. When grateful people gave more money, it showed up on the fMRI scans as greater neural sensitivity in the medial prefrontal cortex.

Another component had participants writing gratitude letters. The gratitude letter writers showed greater activation in the medial prefrontal cortex when they experienced gratitude. (Which was confirmed with an fMRI scanner.) This effect was found three months after the letter writing began, which may indicate that simply expressing gratitude may have lasting positive effects on the brain. This finding suggests that practicing gratitude may help train the brain to be more sensitive to the experience of gratitude down the line, and this could contribute to improved mental health over *time*.

Think It and Ink it

There are many ways to get into that gracious, gratitude feeling. But one that I really love is where you create lists in your gratitude journal or workbook. I discussed this technique in detail in the chapter on Powerful, Important, Morning Practices. Take your body's rhythms into account as you spend the time on this. Are you a morning person or a night person? The goal is to establish a routine at the same time every day so that it becomes part of your self-care practice.

Gratitude Exercise Review

Get your journal and grab a pen, right now. Or go to www.adesignedlifellc.com and download the Gratitude Exercise. Write down five things that you have in your life that you are grateful for today. That's it. Put that journal and pen beside your bed to read tomorrow morning. When you wake up, start your morning by reading your list of the five gratitude's and add one more to it. Do this every day for thirty days. Remember, you cannot repeat anything that you have already written on that list. It might look like this:

Monday—*I am grateful for…*

1. *My bed*
2. *My silver bracelet*
3. *My coffeemaker*
4. *My job*
5. *My feeling rested.*

Tuesday—*I am grateful for my bed, my silver bracelet, my coffeemaker, my job, my feeling rested, and my sister.*

I am grateful for…

6. My bed
7. My silver bracelet
8. My coffeemaker
9. My job
10. My feeling rested.
11. My amazing sister

Every day, you have to read the list and add a new gratitude.

As you get into the habit of gratitude, reading and re-reading your own grateful thoughts, you start being grateful for even the smallest things. You are training your brain to look for reasons to be grateful. The other day, I was grateful that I had a charger on my desk that works and plugs into my Mac. I am not kidding, because I had to find *something*. And that was it. Now, every time I look at that cord, I know that it will click into place, it doesn't have to be jiggled, and it doesn't need tape around it like my other one—I am so grateful for that. See? We can be grateful for even the smallest things.

If you haven't tried a gratitude practice, now is the time to start. Could you imagine what your experience would be like in the morning if you sat there and read twenty things you were grateful for? As your list grows, you would have to dig deep to find another. It's the effort of digging deep that will make your vibration better. It's more work that will lead to more results as your vibration is coming up.

Chapter 11
THE ROAD AHEAD

And when things start to happen, don't worry. Don't stew. Just go right along. You'll start happening, too.

Dr. Seuss

A Bump in the Road

When I talk to clients, there comes a point in their journey where life throws a new obstacle in their path. It could be a mild to a moderate crisis, like finding out their company is closing the branch where they work, or it could be an awesome opportunity—but whatever it is, it throws an unexpected monkey wrench in the plans that they had put in place. They call me up, saying, "Sam, something's wrong. I feel like I'm losing momentum. I don't know what's going on with me." "It's okay," I tell them. "It's just time for a tune-up."

I used to have a car that was psychic. I called it the "Psychic Operational Sedan", or POS for short. (Okay, it may not have been *psychic*, but it was definitely a *POS!*) Somehow, whenever my bank account was starting to look too full, my "psychic car" could tell that I was thinking about spending this surplus cash on something fun and immediately has a breakdown. Eventually, I got a better car, but I learned that whatever vehicle I have, the way to avoid the psychic car phenomenon is by paying to maintain it throughout the year. I stopped ignoring the little warning signals and started doing regular preventative maintenance. I would get little noises checked out instead of turning up the radio. I booked oil changes and annual tune-ups.

So, how do you plan for tune-ups in your life? You plan for them by recognizing that they are necessary. You plan for them by recognizing that if you disconnect from the work and start coasting, you will lose momentum. You put in the work to get here; don't give up now!

It's like you've been going to the gym for so many months, working out, and getting strong. Then you go on a vacation or take a break and get out of the habit of regular workouts. What happens is during that extended time away you gradually lose muscle strength until you notice that you have to exert yourself carrying a double load of groceries. "This is harder work than I remember it being," you say. We've all been there. If you stop building that muscle, it will atrophy.

There are warning signs that will alert you if you pay attention. Your clothes don't fit as well. You're not sleeping as well. You realize, okay, I got these killer results because I was committed. It's not magic. It's not going to stay that way unless you keep working on the process. You have to stay in some kind of maintenance mode.

Make sure to keep up your daily practice to stay in maintenance mode. Keep a P.I.M.P. going. If you feel bored, change it up! It's your meditation. Maybe you'll even look at your calendar and say, "What am I going to do this year?" and calendarize when you are changing a P.I.M.P.

For instance, I started a new P.I.M.P. a couple of months ago. I don't always do it on the calendar change; sometimes I just do it when I think it's a good idea. I don't always wait for the new year. That's kind of like waiting for Monday to re-start a diet.

There's nothing wrong with making resolutions, but only eight percent of people achieve their New Year's resolutions. That means ninety-two percent fail at their New Year's resolutions.

When you are noticing symptoms of your dissatisfaction, such as not feeling well physically, being unmotivated, and feeling a little blue or discontented, it could be that some things are starting to get a little out of control. These are little tell-tale signs that you need to start working on your practice again. I think when you start saying, "My life is getting out of control," you've definitely done more than slip. You need to start paying attention immediately.

If you ignore those earlier signs that I just shared, they'll get bigger and louder. They will start showing up as physical pain. They will start manifesting, trying to get your attention. They will start manifesting in relationship problems, job problems, and money problems. Things will go back to the way they were if you completely disconnect.

Those paradigms, as I said before, are sneaky little bitches. They are just sitting around, waiting for you to slip—they are just looking for their opportunity—and they will try and find their way in again. When you had a very strong practice, they couldn't find their way in. But if you are slipping, they start looking for cracks.

So, how are we going to stop those paradigms from finding cracks? Do I recommend that you sign up for a course every month for the rest of your life? Not necessarily, unless that's your thing. Recently, I started reading one personal development book each month (or listening to the audiobook), at minimum, outside of my normal work.

Now, you have to understand that I listen to my thought leaders. I listen to podcasts, lectures, and TED Talks all the time. I've already put a lot of energy into this practice. If you are just starting this as an entirely new practice for yourself, that might be like trying to lift 270 pounds when you should be starting off with 10 or 15 pounds.

Let's think of it this way. Reading this book is just the tip of the iceberg. Not that we are sick, but no one is going to be cured because they read one book. Rather, it's in how you begin to implement the practices that you've learned.

I wrote this blog a while back.

Is Disconnecting from Everything Really a Good Thing?

Is disconnecting from everything really a good thing? I think not! Hear me out here. For the last several summers I have designed my online coaching business to slow down so I could travel with my family and create great memories. I purposely cut down my usual schedule of 25–30 hours a week to 2–3 hours a day, four days a week. I coach in the morning from wherever I am (this summer it is six weeks in the North Western United States and British Columbia, Canada)

It is a time to soak up all those things that we miss while living full-time in our Mexican paradise, such as the moderate weather, virtual reality gaming, professional sporting events, hiking, boating, science centers, urban landmarks, and enjoying some of our favorite restaurants and spirits. We had lots of rest and downtime as well. This list is long and impressive.

So, why was I fighting anxiety? I noticed I was struggling to feel grounded and good. I had all this amazing stuff around me, by my creation and choice, and I was having a great time with family and friends, so what was happening? Then I realized AHA, that it is what I haven't been doing. I had not been maintaining the amazing stuff that is within me. I had disconnected a bit too much from Source, from my internal and spiritual daily work.

One morning after a very big day of emotional and even physical discomfort, I started to listen. I really didn't have a choice. I became that uncomfortable. My hips were hurting, I had acid reflux, and I was reacting rather than responding to an unexpected, disappointing, and stressful situation. It was awful. Yuckville for sure. I jumped in the hot tub this morning and asked, the question "What is this? What is this yuck that I am feeling?" And right away, loud and clear, I got my answer: "You have disconnected from Source." (Yes, we all know, ultimately, one is always connected.)

However, I knew what this answer meant. I was not attending to my self-care or even sort of maintaining my internal work. I had stopped listening to great thought leaders, reading the things that constantly remind me of all that I am, all that I have, and all that I am capable of. I had stopped my powerful, important, morning practice (P.I.M.P.). I was taking a break from the work. BAD IDEA... On top of all that, as I mentioned earlier, I was indulging in restaurants and spirits. Prosecco, in excess, of course, caused the acid reflux. Just a yummy bagel roll at the famous German Restaurant, or the breading on fresh fried West Coast oysters for the gluten sensitive like myself, will ruin a day (or week). For us? It is like just a little bit of poison. I know this! But yet, I just turned off some things that I know are in my best interest, practices that keep me in an incredible vibration.

So, is completely disconnecting a good thing? I THINK NOT! Just writing this has bumped my frequency so much, and things that were worrying me yesterday have easily been resolved in my head. (That is, after all, where we do the most damage and the most work.) I am still on holiday and, as a matter of fact, I have been writing this while going between the steam room, jacuzzi, cold shower, and dry sauna in my hotel in Vancouver, B.C.

Today is a beautiful day and I am so full of gratitude. I have put the stress and BS into perspective. I noticed, I asked, I listened, and

I got back into a great frequency. All good!

Ps. Yes, even life coaches have slips.

(Buckley-Hugessen 2018)

Defuse the Disconnect

I want my summers to disconnect from things because this is work. Nobody said that having a good life wasn't work! It's the same thing as going to the gym. It's the same thing as eating all-natural foods. Anything that you are doing that's good for you is work. It doesn't have to be hard, but you're smoking crack if you don't think this is work.

Often, when I have disconnected in the past, I would let paradigms run the show. For example, I wouldn't listen to a podcast or read a book. Or I would just want to eat really fattening foods and sleep in. I finally learned that I can't do any of that. I will get sick from doing that. I will get physically sick. I will also be off my game, mentally. I will get those signs really fast, such as feeling a little bit blue and anxious.

We already know that *how* is none of our business. It's nobody's business on the how. We find ourselves back into noticing problems rather than knowing their solutions.

Defuse the disconnect by planning for it—just know it's going to happen. Put it into a calendar and decide that maybe in the third quarter or the third month of the year that you are going to look for a course. Or maybe decide that you are going to read a spiritually uplifting book each month that is all about filling you up. Taking it to the next level, maybe your next step is to hire a coach. Maybe it's finding a really great accountability partner who knows the work that you have committed to.

Don't burn yourself out by taking your "recharge time" out of your schedule. That is how you suck the fun out of your life! And we're not letting the paradigms win, right?

I can tell you that it was after just taking the summer off, I was having so much fun with my kids, exploring, hiking, and doing healthy things, but they weren't things I needed to do—that I let the disconnect become my habit. I was overindulging. I was eating food that I missed, so to speak. I started feeling all of those things I mentioned, such as anxiety and physical illness. That's when I said to myself, "Okay, lean back in. Obviously, there's an in-moderation component. You can't just disconnect without setting parameters."

Remember, all you have to do is start. In my case, I got out the book, *Think and Grow Rich* by Napoleon Hill. I committed to reading that book, and then I got another book and committed to completing that one. That's how I did it. I got off my sucky paradigm-fest-and got back to listening to my thought leaders and listening to my podcasts. Start where you are and get back on the horse. That's how you do it.

The Accountability Advantage

I'm taking Spanish lessons, and my Spanish teacher will tell you that I'm doing great. But you know what? I don't want to. It's work, and I just want to know Spanish, I don't want to do the work. It's like I just want to have the happy feeling of knowing another language, but I don't want to do the work. Or, you might find yourself asking (like me), if I already did the work, why is it slipping?

This is what I know: I have to go back to heavy lifting, so guess what? Instead of quitting Spanish lessons, I just set them up for twice a week. I am committed and accountable to my Spanish coach. I know that if you give me a week where I don't *have* to study, I will take all week to *not* study. I find a lot of my clients are like that, too. I think I am a great coach for them, but I'm also a huge accountability partner. My clients know that if they are scheduled to meet me on Monday at 9:00 a.m., I will want to know what progress they have made over the week. They are up until midnight Sunday doing their lifework. Good intentions are not as powerful motivators as the reluctance we feel to let others down.

When you start noticing that things are slipping, and you are feeling disconnected, lean in right away. Don't wait for it to get bad, and definitely don't wait for it to go back to your lowest point, because it will go back. You don't need that to happen again! If you began a fitness routine to train for a marathon, you don't give up all your efforts after a weekend getaway with your friends. Just like if you stop doing crunches, you're going to get belly fat. Your abs will become flabs.

Are you feeling nervous that you will be caught right back in the same old stuckness that you were in before? Yes, it's possible, but you are not going to let that happen, are you? That is why there is need for accountability. Getting someone who will hold you to your word is critical. Having accountability gives you the strength to follow through on the difficult work. That's the thing, it's work—but the payoff is amazing. It's such small work, compared to the giant, humongous reward.

You better work! -**RuPaul Charles**

I'm not going to lie to you here, there isn't a finish line. You're not cured, I'm not cured. This is a constant process. Think of your progress like a precious stone that you are polishing, or like restoring a classic car. At first, you just care about getting the parts to get the motor running. Then, you work on getting it roadworthy. It's not constantly working against decay, but you can see the next level, the places where you can improve it some more.

Yes, if you let things go and ignore warning signals, it could decay, but you are equipping yourself with tools that will take you higher than before. Rather than constantly running from the paradigms, you're committing to continuous growth. If you continue to grow, the process will become easier. Instead of swinging the steering wheel hard to the left or right, it only takes a gentle nudge to get on course. And here's the main point: we will never perfect ourselves. We were born perfect. I don't know if we are ever going to get back to perfection before we die again. But our soul is perfect, right?

If I start slipping in an area and feel awful as a result, or I start noticing, "okay, I've actually felt like this before,"—and I have felt amazing since that first time, then I know it's not a life sentence. There's no need to panic or beat myself up because I'm back in that place. If anything, I can take it as a sign that I am ready to level up! I love to remind myself that I have evidence that I have risen before. I *know* change is possible because I have created x, y, z in my life since the last time I felt this way. And here's the good news: it won't take as long. If I've done it once, I can do it again. I know I am absolutely capable of creating it again. I have evidence and proof. Your proof is that you already did it.

Remember, it's not like you are powerless in this; you have a lot of power. You are capable of doing many *great* things if you are willing to trust and move forward, one baby step at a time. We have to remind ourselves of that. I remind myself of how I started out. Remember, at the beginning of this book, when we talked about hormones and how terrible I felt? And guess what, hormones are sneaky too. They show up and try and pull tricks to get me stuck in a place of low vibrations. I tell myself, "Okay, you know what? I've felt amazing since this first started, and I'm going to feel amazing again. We are just going to find the solutions. We are just going to lean in."

When you have a car, you have to put gas in it. And every once in a while, you stop at the service station and change the oil. When it's caked with salt, dirt, and sand, you run it through the car wash and vacuum it out. Give it some attention. The car wasn't broken; it just needed some attention. It's the same with us. You're not broken, and I'm not broken; we just need a little attention in certain areas. We got too busy to do our maintenance.

What do we do? REVIEW! We go back to our P.I.M.P. We go back to adding something new to strip off the old paradigms that found their way back into our life. Sign up for a new course, take yoga, or commit to reading one book a month. Find an accountability partner who is going to hold your feet to the fire and stick with you until you get unstuck! Hire a coach. Go back and calendarize your check-ins. Roll up your sleeves and grab a ponytail elastic because it's time for you to pull up your messy bun and get shit done!

Chapter 12
SO, WHAT DO YOU KNOW?

There are two primary choices in life: to accept conditions as they exist, or accept the responsibility for changing them
Denis Waitley

At a certain point in my workshops, I see people nodding as if they are thinking, "Yes, Sam, I'm getting it now." That's when I know it's time to flip the script and encourage them to assess what they've learned. Here we are, at the beginning. And the end is the beginning. You've got your tools; they are all here. So, let's take it home. Now, it's your turn to think about these questions: What landed for you? What did you learn? What's your takeaway?

What are your takeaways from these ten prior chapters? What did you learn and what did you apply? (Go to www.adesignedlifellc.com to download)

I learned…_____

_____

_____

_____

_____

How did it show up in your life?

_____
_____
_____
_____

What are you committing to doing differently moving forward?

_____
_____
_____

Write three new practices that you will commit to in your life. (Some examples might be: yoga, breathing, reading, hiring a coach, meditating, doing your LOVE/NOT IT list every year, and re-writing your vision your dream.)

I am committed to…_____
_____
_____
_____
_____
_____

By the way, go back and re-write your LOVEs and NOT ITs because there have definitely been some shifts in them. I've yet to meet one person that wrote it and didn't re-write it within the first three months. Sometimes, when you begin a list of what you love, you find yourself making lists of things that you know would make your mother happy if she ever read them (or your boss, or even a romantic partner!). Consider if you're writing the list for someone else who may have been riding along in your head. Don't write what you think "should" be on the list to please someone else. That won't be what you truly LOVE.

LOVE/NOT IT

I LOVE...

_____
_____
_____
_____
_____

_____

NOT IT:

_____
_____
_____
_____
_____

_____

Your Vision Story

Wanna make a bet? By now you've stopped reading your vision story that you wrote at the beginning of the book, haven't you? It's okay. There's a reason that can happen. For example, I took on three new clients at a time when I had no room for any more. I took them all on within two weeks of each other. They are very, very, strong personalities. Two of them took the LOVE/NOT IT assignment in a completely different direction than I had intended.

The way they wrote their vision and story was very much like a story that they would be publishing—it was very theatrical. Each one was full of buzz words like, "I envision myself becoming one with the universe and knowing my divine self." WTF, dude? That is great and all but I knew better, I have been doing this work a long time. What made it doubly crazy because these were all business clients!

When they wrote their vision, they wrote what they thought I wanted to hear. They wrote what they thought would sound good to me. I could tell immediately when I read their vision stories that they were in "people pleasing mode" and I sent them all back to the drawing board. I had to tell them, "Sorry, guys, but there is zero charge in this. I feel zero charge, you are not committed to this. This is not your wow." That's not what they wanted to hear!

But I had each client re-write their vision, based only on the facts. What would you love? What is showing up as NOT IT? Really, what is it? If it's "I don't want to work sixty hours a week," then excellent; what would you love instead?

Their visions had to change. Many clients come to me for a fresh take on their work and realize that they want to quit their jobs. Sometimes big corporations are reluctant to hire me because I'm going to get people functioning in their true purpose, what they are really great at, and what they love, and it might not be sitting behind a desk in an office cubicle.

A word of advice as you write your vision story: human nature typically wants to do everything perfectly, without going through the *process* of improvement. That's often where procrastination comes from. Sometimes it's just being lazy, but other times it's wanting to wait until the conditions and the circumstances are perfect. Or, it's the fear of disappointing others.

Here's a message that I hope we've hit home in this book: *do it imperfectly*. We forget that false starts and missteps are part of the process. You don't have to get it exactly right, but you do have to start. Do it imperfectly and take a little action every day. Doing nothing is not an option. It's okay to re-write your vision.

This is how we learn and how we grow. I promise it's going to be fine.

Now that you have had time to think more about what you love, I guarantee that some things have changed for you. I've been doing this long enough that I know without a doubt some things have changed. Roll it around in your head again. Let's redo this now and propel you.

Do you know what the good news is? Some things have already been attained. Some things have already happened. The Universe heard them, it rushed in, and it's now okay, I already have that. The manifestation of that might be the car, the house, and other material things, or it might be a leap forward in your health.

It's time to write YOUR NEW STORY. We are going to get this out. It's time to ink it, not just think it.

In my typical morning, I wake up and_____
_____
_____
_____

I'm so glad I get to_____
_____
_____
_____

My typical day looks like_____
_____
_____
_____

In the evening, I like to_____
_____
_____
_____

I am surrounded by some pretty amazing people, such as_____
_____
_____
_____
_____
_____

I am committed to taking care of myself so that I can_____
_____
_____
_____

Something I love about my life is_____
_____
_____
_____

_____
_____

I am so appreciative that_____
_____
_____
_____

When you are writing, you have to think in large concepts, what your life looks like once you have moved "Up-level". Because, typically, when we start this visioning process, we play it small. We treat our visions more like goals. These are dreams; you are not supposed to know how to get them. They are big and yummy.

If you are having difficulty getting started with your vision/story, try thinking about what advice would your future self give to you right now about the work that you have done? Your future self has the life that they designed; they have done the work and stayed connected.

What advice would that future self give you right now? Life totally worked out, you are totally free and unstuck, what does that person tell you right now? Write it down, and date it.

_____
_____
_____
_____
_____
_____

Date_____

Put it on your calendar to make a date with yourself to come back in three months and test whether or not you are on the right track.

Now that you have followed the recipe and used all the ingredients listed, how are the cookies?

Here is to getting Unstuck and designing a life you love.

Love,

Sam

BIBLIOGRAPHY

Buckley-Hugessen, Samantha. 2018. "Coach Finder Online -blog." *Coachfinderonline.com.* August 6. Accessed June 24, 2019. https://coachfinderonline.com/is-disconnecting-from-everything-really-a-good-thing/.

2017. "Greater Good Magazine." *Greater Good Science Center, at UC Berkeley University.* June 6. Accessed June 24, 2019. https://greatergood.berkeley.edu/article/item/how_gratitude_changes_you_and_your_brain.

2014. "Healthbeat." *Harvard Health Publishing, Harvard Medical School.* November. https://www.health.harvard.edu/healthbeat/giving-thanks-can-make-you-happier.

Ready, Keith. 2015. "A Gift of Inspiration -InspirEmail #289." *A Gift of Inspiration.com.* March. Accessed June 24, 2019. http://www.agiftofinspiration.com.au/stories/attitude/hotdogs.shtml.

Yetman, David. 2016. "More Money Was Made During the Great Depression." *Century 21.ca.* January 17. Accessed June 24, 2019. https://www.century21.ca/david.yetman/blog/More_Money_was_Made_During_the_Great_Depression.

BOOK SUMMARY

Once upon a time, there was a little version of you. A perfect little you who chased big dreams, believed in fairytales and wanted a life filled with fun and adventure. Barefoot and laughing, bursting with anticipation, that child had a mind like an open book made of blank pages. The book of your life was waiting to be filled with colorful stories and effervescent experiences.

Isn't that how all of our lives begin?

Before too long, that book gets pushed aside and pushed aside, until it's virtually been forgotten about, with its pages crumpled and torn.

Perhaps it took years for that book to become a distant memory. Maybe one violently unhappy chapter in your younger life stole that book out of your little hands and tarnished it so badly that you don't dare open the cover to look into it again.

Before you know it, life enveloped you like quicksand and here you are today – entrenched in an existence that you didn't choose for yourself. Or at least, you don't want to admit that you chose. Life grabbed you by the bits and has you feeling crappy and truly stuck.

Being stuck SUCKS! That was originally going to be in the title of this book. But actually, helping people find a solution was my goal of writing it, not to point out the obvious. But I will say it again, being stuck DOES SUCK.

Maybe you're stuck in a relationship that's not feeding your soul or stuck in a job that brings you nothing but stress and boredom. Perhaps your business has been slowly sucking all your time and energy away from you while not paying you an income that you so rightly deserve.

Or maybe you're in some warped version of Groundhog Day where the best part of your day is binge-watching Netflix while stuffing down a liter of Haagen-Dazs.

Sound familiar?

Then you, my friend, are completely STUCK.

There's nothing cool about living a mediocre life. There's nothing rewarding about simply surviving. And I guarantee you that there's not a soul on this earth who wished he or she had watched more television or worked an extra shift when they're on their deathbed.

The sad truth is – few of us actually do any more than just exist in this lifetime.

We get by.

We simply do what we can to get through each day.

And perhaps even more frighteningly, we often live our lives based on what other people tell us we're supposed to be doing!

Seriously?? Can't we do better than 'getting by?' Can't we live a life that we leap out of bed each morning feeling enthused, challenged and invigorated? Often if not always?

Oh, I hear what you're thinking: 'but I can't just do whatever I want. I have kids, I have responsibilities, I'm in debt up to my eyeballs.'

The list of 'I can't', 'I shouldn't' and 'I don't know's' are coursing through your brain like a freight train right about now.

As a life coach and mentor for many years now, I can tell you that I have heard them all. Excuses and false beliefs pour out of people like molten lava when asked what they would LOVE to do with their life – engulfing and destroying everything living thing as they go.

How do you know if you're stuck?

If you find yourself answering 'I don't know' repeatedly to others when asked the simple question 'What do YOU love?' or asking yourself how you got yourself into this mess of a life over and over again, then friend - I ask you – no, I BEG you to stop what you're doing and read this book.

I promise you - you CAN pull yourself out of the sucky stuckness that you're currently in.

This book doesn't have anything inside of it that your inner self doesn't already deeply understand. It gives you an opportunity to dial back into the yearnings that you've shelved away for a rainy day and calls upon you to hear them and then take action. I promise, it is completely and totally possible for you to UNS*UCK Yourself and live a life you love.

Xo

Sam

MEET SAMANTHA

Like you, Samantha is made up of many parts, including her professional self, her family relationships and the person she inside.

Career-wise Samantha is a Certified Professional Coach with 30+ years of Sales, Sales Management and Training experience in Resort real estate sales, weight loss and other non-tangible sales industries. Always recognized as a force to be reckoned with in the sales world, with dozens of top performer awards, Samantha chose to redesign her career mid-life to fulfil her true passion as a Coach, Mentor and to develop people full time.

Samantha, the person, is a dedicated wife and mother who knows what it is like to feel stuck. She is a fun, loving, kind person who swears sometimes, often, okay A LOT, but who also understands what it is like to be depressed and anxious.

She has also:

- Been really transparent.
- Grieved over lost loved ones.
- Spent many, many sessions in therapy.
- Raised herself in an extremely dysfunctional home.

www.ingramcontent.com/pod-product-compliance
Lightning Source LLC
LaVergne TN
LVHW011942070526
838202LV00054B/4756